/ 25

THE
AFRICAN
ELEPHANT

TWILIGHT IN EDEN

THE AFRICAN ELEPHANT

TWILIGHT IN EDEN

A NATIONAL AUDUBON SOCIETY BOOK

Roger L. DiSilvestro

Christopher N. Palmer
EXECUTIVE EDITOR

Page Chichester
PHOTOGRAPHER

JOHN WILEY & SONS, INC.

New York ▮ Chichester ▮ Brisbane ▮ Toronto ▮ Singapore

Wiley Staff
Editor: David Sobel
Managing Editor: Frank Grazioli

The African Elephant was designed by Stanley S. Drate/ Folio Graphics Co., Inc.
Cover Design: Laurie Angel-Sadis

If you would like to receive information about the National Audubon Society write to:
National Audubon Society
Membership Department
950 Third Avenue
New York, NY 10022

Library of Congress Cataloging-in-Publication Data

DiSilvestro, Roger L.
    The African elephant : twilight in Eden / Roger L. DiSilvestro;
  executive editor, Christopher N. Palmer; principal photographer,
  Page Chichester.
      p.   cm.
  Includes bibliographical references and index.
  ISBN 0-471-53207-X
    1. African elephant. 2. Wildlife conservation. I. Palmer,
  Christopher N. II. Title.
  QL737.P98D57   1991
333.95'9—dc20   90-24967
                                                 CIP

Printed in the United States of America

91 92   10 9 8 7 6 5 4 3 2 1

■

For
Joseph DiSilvestro
Lee Chichester
and Gail Shearer

■

ACKNOWLEDGMENTS

For their help in reviewing the manuscript and honing its accuracy we owe special thanks to Richard Leakey, head of Kenya's Wildlife Services; Elizabeth McCorkle, coordinator for the African Wildlife Foundation's elephant campaign; Diana McMeekin, vice-president of the African Wildlife Foundation; Mike Sutton, World Wildlife Fund expert on the ivory trade, and Audubon staff members Fran Spivey-Weber and Dorie Bolze.

A special, heartfelt thanks goes to Isabella Rossellini, John Lithgow, and James Earl Jones for their help in behalf of the African elephant as the stars of *The Last Elephant,* the National Audubon Society's first wildlife drama. We at Audubon firmly believe that fictional feature films based on the drama of real-life conservation dramas are a potent new means for bringing the conservation message to a vast new audience.

For their help during the African phase of this book's production we also owe thanks to elephant biologists Iain Douglas-Hamilton, Barbara McKnight, Cynthia Moss, and Joyce Poole; John Donaldson, of Black, Manafort, Stone, and Kelly; Patrick Hamilton, senior warden at Tsavo National Park; Samuel M. Kisiki, a research biologist and assistant warden at Tsavo National Park; Peter Nganga, a Kenya wildlife ranger; Perez Olindo, former director of Kenya's Wildlife Conservation and Management Department; Nehemiah K. arap Rotich, executive director of the East African Wildlife Society; Daphne Sheldrick, who has spent decades caring for orphaned baby elephants; David Western, chairman of the African Elephant and Rhino Specialist Group; and William Woodley, senior warden in charge of antipoaching operations at Tsavo National Park. For their seemingly never-ending work at keeping our book projects going, we owe hearty thanks to National Audubon Society Productions' office staff—production coordinator Delores Simmons and our assistant Ruth Thomas.

CHRISTOPHER N. PALMER
ROGER L. DiSILVESTRO
PAGE CHICHESTER

FOREWORD

In the past ten years alone, the world has stood witness to a 50-percent decline in the number of African elephants. In 1979 the continental population was estimated at 1.3 million. By 1989 the figure had plummeted to 609,000, and it was belatedly acknowledged that the international ivory trade was primarily responsible for the rapid decline. But the numbers do not tell the whole story. In areas of heavy poaching, the big breeding males have been relentlessly pursued for their heavier tusks. Matriarchs, too, have been gunned down, families fragmented, and orphans left to die without the care and companionship of their relatives. If these trends were to continue, the African elephant, the largest animal to walk the Earth since prehistoric times, would be pushed toward extinction by the turn of the century.

The loss of the elephant would be a great human tragedy, for elephants inspire the respect of all who come into close contact with them. Perhaps these feelings arise because elephants have so many of the characteristics that we most admire in ourselves: great power, strength, and dignity; compassion, loyalty, and cooperation; and the formation of life-long friendships. Those who have lived closely with elephants would say that they have a sense of humour and a sense of self, and no one would doubt that they have an eerie sense of death.

Hunters and early naturalists remarked on the uncanny ability of elephants to communicate with one another over long distances and believed that they used some sort of extrasensory perception. Biologists have only recently discovered that, in addition to a complex vocal repertoire of audible trumpets and roars and rumbles, elephants do have a kind of ESP or "secret language." Many of the calls used by elephants are infrasonic (below the level of human hearing) or have infrasonic components, and elephants use some of these vocalizations to call back and forth to one another over distances of several kilometers. It is ironic that in some areas African elephants have been brought to the brink of extinction just as we are learning so much about their complex social behavior and communication.

Over the past few years, we have heard more about the plight of the elephant than perhaps about any other single species. Elephant badges and bumper stickers, elephant articles, books, and television specials abound. All of this clamor begs the question: Why do we care? Why save the elephant at all? There are different answers for different people. Some would say that elephants have an intrinsic value and that the mere existence of elephants enriches their lives. Others feel that elephants are valuable only insofar as they are useful to human beings. Both answers are legitimate. The intrinsic value we place on elephants may be generated by an empathy, by our ability to identify with elephants because they have behavioral characteristics similar to our own. We also value elephants as an essential link in many ecosystems. The disappearance of the elephant in some areas could lead to biological impoverishment and loss of biodiversity. Furthermore, as a large, charismatic mammal, the elephant can be successfully used to engender financial support for many of our national parks and reserves and for the other less popular species that live within them. Finally we value elephants economically: alive they are an important source of income from tourism in some African countries; dead they provide revenue from skins, meat, and ivory.

In a perfect world, where it was possible to distinguish a tusk from an elephant who died a natural death or was killed legally from one that was killed illegally, few would find fault with a continuing ivory trade. But unfortunately, the situation is not that simple. Despite all the regulations, restrictions, and quotas enacted by CITES (Convention on International Trade in Endangered Species), by 1989 approximately 80 percent of the ivory traded within the "legal" CITES system was actually derived from illegally killed elephants. Many people believed that yet another compromise solution would sacrifice the remaining African elephants and that placing an international ban on the ivory trade was the only way to slow the devastating declines in elephant numbers.

In October 1989, after much heated debate, the seventh conference of the parties to CITES voted to upgrade the African elephant from Appendix II to Appendix I, a move that bans all international commercial trade in ivory and other elephant products. But the ban is just one battle in a war that we must continue to fight if we are to save the Earth's largest land mammal. There are many countries that are not party to the CITES agreement, and there are others that refuse to comply with the ban.

To protect elephant populations over the long-term will require a broadly integrated approach to conservation. As long as there is an ivory trade, significant sums of money will need to be spent on anti-poaching campaigns in Africa. Measures will need to be taken to ensure that the international ivory trade ban is enforced. In addition, if viable populations of elephants are to survive, they will need the support and cooperation of the people with whom they share their land. The people who suffer the *costs* of elephants on their land need to realize *benefits* from such wildlife. Protecting elephant populations will also require better monitoring and research. Finally elephant conservation will not be effective without widespread awareness of the problems that elephants face.

For the African elephant to live through the twenty-first century, a level of global cooperation unprecedented in the sphere of species conservation will be required. The countries that are home to the elephant will need to organize more effective law enforcement and better wildlife conservation policies, while the consumer countries must continue to reduce their demand for ivory and increase their financial assistance to the wildlife departments of African countries.

As individuals there is much that you can do: don't buy, wear, display, or sell ivory. If there is little or no global demand, the price of ivory will continue to decline and there will be little incentive for poachers to kill elephants. But as long as people around the world are willing to buy ivory, poachers will risk their lives to kill elephants. You can also help by learning about elephants and passing on what you know to your friends.

Much was accomplished for elephant conservation in 1989, and there are grand plans for the next decade. We have won a battle, but we still have a long fight ahead to secure the elephant's future and win the ivory war. To use a Kenyan expression, saving the elephant will require a *harambee* spirit: we will need to work together if we are to save the African elephant for our children's grandchildren to enjoy.

RICHARD E. LEAKEY
JOYCE POOLE
NAIROBI, KENYA

PRESIDENT'S STATEMENT
by Peter A. A. Berle
President, National Audubon Society

The plight of the African elephant as ivory poachers threatened to shoot it into extinction captured the imagination, concern, and chagrin of the world. Thanks to the dedicated work of conservationists around the globe, trade in elephant ivory has been banned and the poacher's guns are being silenced. For the moment it appears that the elephant may be permitted to recover. However, the danger to the elephant will be revived if trade in ivory ever resumes. The National Audubon Society offers this book as part of its effort to keep the elephant a vital part of public and political concern and to provide insight into the threats still faced by the African elephant.

PREFACE
Christopher N. Palmer
President, National Audubon Society Productions, Inc.

Sweeping changes in the world's political and economic landscape have raised environmental issues to a high priority on the world agenda. This visibility is badly needed because environmental problems are challenging us on every front. Climate change, ozone depletion, soil erosion, deforestation, water scarcity, toxic contamination, air pollution, and overpopulation are only some of the problems that are becoming so severe that they threaten human society.

The National Audubon Society is using science, policy research, lobbying, education, litigation, and citizen action to tackle these environmental problems. With the support of more than 600,000 members and an extensive chapter network in the United States and Latin America, the National Audubon Society draws on the enthusiasm and power of its grassroots constituency to save wildlife habitat and other fragile natural resources. On many important issues, from the protection of forests and wetlands to the battle against global warming, Audubon works to influence key decision-makers at all levels of government, from local zoning boards to the United Nations.

The National Audubon Society manages and protects a nationwide system of wildlife sanctuaries on which Audubon and outside experts conduct field research, restore natural systems, and demonstrate clean, sustainable resource management. Audubon also reaches out to the broader public through its well-known Audubon TV Specials and through a special educational effort in inner-city classrooms.

This book by Roger L. DiSilvestro, chief staff writer for National Audubon Society Productions, is a reflection of Audubon's interest in international issues. We are an international organization.

The idea for this book was born when we launched a successful effort to produce film dramas with strong environmental themes. By producing entertaining fictional films based on scientific data and real-world problems, we hope to bring the environmental message to a vast new audience. The number of environmental threats the world faces is alarming, yet millions of people are ignorant of how their lives and livelihood are being jeopardized by these threats. New educational strategies that can reach audiences that have minimal interest in environmental issues are urgently needed. The Motion Picture Association of America reports that on average every U.S. citizen goes to a film theater more than four times each year. It is essential that environmentalists use this valuable medium.

Roger L. DiSilvestro created the storyline for our first film, which focused on the poaching of the African elephant. The result was a movie called *The Last*

Elephant, starring John Lithgow, Isabella Rossellini, and James Earl Jones. It aired on prime-time television in the United States, thanks to Ted Turner and Turner Network Television, and was released theatrically overseas. You can find it now in home-video stores. It is aimed at the millions of people who are unfamiliar with the plight of the African elephant and who may unthinkingly buy ivory trinkets and jewelry from gift shops, fashion boutiques, and department stores.

The African elephant, as Roger DiSilvestro makes clear in this book, is in a fight for survival, and we hope this book will help it win that fight. The African Wildlife Foundation reported recently that at the height of the ivory trade in the late 1980s, poachers slaughtered one African elephant every five and a half minutes. One solution to this problem is to reduce permanently the worldwide demand for ivory.

Since an almost worldwide ban on trade in ivory went into effect in 1990, poaching has declined and the price of ivory has collapsed. But there is pressure to reverse the ban, so we cannot relax. We need a *permanent* drop in the world market, and for this to happen we need an informed citizenry. We believe that no one who reads this book or watches *The Last Elephant* will buy ivory or approve of its sale. But the threats to elephant survival go beyond even the ivory trade. If the ivory war is won, even tougher challenges loom ahead, as outlined in this book. The key to elephant survival, as indeed to our own, is a complete understanding of environmental problems.

An ancient Chinese proverb says:

> If you plan for a year, plant rice.
> If you plan for ten years, plant trees.
> If you plan for a century, educate your children.

If we want our society, and the wild places and things we hold dear, to survive the environmental challenges we now face, we have to plan for 100 years. We think this book will bring an important message to both you and your children. Thanks for reading it.

CONTENTS

EARLY HISTORY:
ELEPHANTS,
ROMANS, GREEKS,
AND VICTORIANS

I had seen a herd of elephants travelling through dense native forest, pacing along as if they had an appointment at the end of the world.

Karen Blixen, *Out of Africa*

∎

A nimals manifested mental phenomena long before man existed . . . the elephant prefigured the sagacity of the human mind.

Robert Chambers, *Vestiges of the Natural History of Creation*

∎

H ad we known no other animate life-form than our own, we should have been utterly mysterious to ourselves as a species.

Mary Midgley, *Beast & Man: The Roots of Human Nature*

∎

DEEP IN THE WARM EARTH OF AFRICA'S MEDITERRA-
nean shores lie the bones of extinct races of elephant,
creatures driven from existence by Romans, Carthaginians, and Egyptians in the time of the pharaohs. In the damp soils
of the Congo rainforests moulder the disarticulated bones of yet
more elephants, remains left by forest-dwelling peoples who
killed the animals with poisoned spears and butchered them for
meat. In the baked soils of South Africa, the bones of long-dead
elephants turn slowly to dust, animals slaughtered in centuries
past to supply the ivory markets and to make the land safe for
farmers.

The association between elephantkind and humankind is ages
old. Our earliest ancestors were nurtured on the flesh of elephants. Millions of years before modern humans burst upon the
evolutionary scene, roving bands of proto-humans butchered
elephant carcasses they found upon the African plains and, with
crude stone-tipped weapons, may have even killed elephants for
food. In later ages, fur-clad races of modern humans hunted the
frozen lands of glaciated Europe, seeking out the African elephant's distant relative and one-time contemporary, the woolly
mammoth. So dependent were these peoples on the mammoths
and other Ice Age creatures for food and hides that when warming periods drove the animals into the far north, the human hunters moved north too. Later still, North American mammoths and
mastodons fell prey to the first settlers of the New World, wandering Asian hunters upon whom an immense misunderstanding
of geography would one day bestow the name *Indians*.

The long association of elephant and human may be finally
drawing to a close. The grasping trunks and deadly tusks that prehistoric hunters and Greek and Roman soldiers faced with trepi-
dation and consummate courage are little threat to modern hunters armed with automatic weapons. Entire herds can be killed to

A young elephant feeds on high grasses near a palm stand.

the last animal within seconds, slain not by hunters in need of food but by profiteers interested only in the ivory, in the elephants' tusks. If the killing were to continue unbridled, the end of this century would mark the end of the African elephant.

∎ ELEPHANT ORIGINS

The story begins about 50 million years ago with animals called moeritheres. The moeritheres were proboscideans, animals with trunks, and four of their incisor teeth—two uppers and two lowers—were incipient tusks. Moeritheres weighed about a quarter ton and were probably amphibious, feeding on plants and living along rivers much as the hippopotamus does today. The moeritheres gave rise within the next 10 million or 20 million years to

tusked creatures that paleontologists have labeled *palaeomastodons*. Some palaeomastodons had both upper and lower tusks, others had only lowers, shaped like shovels.

The next five million years of elephant evolution are lost in the fossil record, but at the end of that gap, mastodons—distant relatives of modern elephants—were roaming across Africa. During the next few million years, mastodons became one of the most common of the large mammals, spreading their numbers all across the world. One early mastodon species was *Gomphotherium*, a four-tusked creature the size of a small African elephant, perhaps 8 feet tall at the shoulder. It was this creature that eventually gave rise to the African elephant we know today. Fossil remains suggest that this apparently was not a big evolutionary step, since the skeletons of African elephants and *Gomphotheria* are much alike. The biggest differences are in the molars and the tusks. The gomphotheres evolved into African elephants, skeletally at least, by losing their lower tusks and by changes in their molars, which became more compact and better adapted to the shearing motion of the elephant's jaws. Elephants' jaws tend to move back and forth when chewing, unlike the more complex rotary movement characteristic of mastodons.

A great bull strides across the Amboseli plain, a sight witnessed since the genesis of the African elephant some 5 million years ago.

This lineage suggests that the African elephant has existed for at least 5 million years, long enough to have observed humankind evolving from a savannah-dwelling, ape-like seeker of plants and animals into a computer-using denizen of the modern urban world. The elephant did not escape the notice of the increasingly technological ape. Paintings and carvings of elephants, even etchings of elephants in ivory, date back at least 30,000 years. In prehistoric Europe, elephants, in the guise of the woolly mammoth, were among the most heavily hunted animals, as proved by the thousands of mammoth bones dug from prehistoric sites in Europe.

The woolly mammoth is perhaps the best known of prehistoric elephants. The fossil record suggests that, like the African elephant, the mammoth was a descendant of the mastodon *Gomphotherium*. Woolly mammoths ranged throughout the chill northern parts of the globe, living in the shadows of the glaciers. They were heavily hunted by groups of Stone Age peoples culturally adapted to preying upon the big mammals that existed during the Ice Ages, such as the woolly rhinoceros and the giant ground sloth. The bones of more than a thousand mammoths were found at a single Stone Age hunting camp excavated by archaeologists in Czechoslovakia. Stone spearheads found among the bones of North American mammoths dating back some 10,000 years show that New World peoples also preyed on mammoths.

A woolly mammoth on the River Somme in prehistoric France, from a detail of a mural by Charles R. Knight. Woolly mammoths were distant relatives of African elephants. They vanished about 5,000 years ago, victims perhaps of changing climates and human hunting.

The mammoth was often featured in prehistoric cave paint-ings and carvings, which is one measure of its importance to Stone Age hunters. The mammoth provided more than meat. Its ivory was used to make statues, etchings, and ornaments; its bones were used for tools and even as building materials for houses, and doubtless its hide was used for clothing and other leather goods.

Mammoth remains provide clues as to how primitive peoples were able to tackle and defeat an animal that stood up to 15 feet tall and was armed with tusks generally 10 to 12 feet long, and sometimes up to 16 feet. At an archaeologic site near Dent, Col-orado, the bones of at least a dozen mammoths were clustered at the mouth of a narrow gully below a cliff, suggesting that hunters had stampeded the animals over the precipice. Stone spear points and large rocks found among the bones indicate how mammoths that survived the fall were dispatched.

At many fossil sites, the bones of mammoths and other large mammals are charred, indicating that they were burned. This sug-gests that prehistoric peoples set fire to woods and grasslands, driving game toward hunters or burning the animals to death. It is also likely that groups of hunters would attack a single mam-moth, circling it as wolves do when attacking a moose, stabbing

A prehistoric mammoth hunt, depicted probably with more imagination than accuracy. Prehistoric peoples were more likely to use spears than arrows and probably hunted in smaller groups.

it with spears in the sides or hindquarters. Stone Age hunters doubtless knew well the effectiveness of hamstringing their large quarry.

Mammoths were dependent on the chill environment created by the glaciers. During warm periods when the glaciers retreated northward, so did the mammoths, with human hunters in tow. When the climate cooled again, glaciers, mammoths, and human hunters would move south. This waxing and waning persisted through four glaciations, each about 50,000 years long, over the course of about a million years. For some unknown reason, the mammoths and many of the other large Ice Age mammals did not survive the next warming period, a period that continues still.

Why the mammoths disappeared is a mystery. They vanished from Europe about 15,000 years ago. In North America they persisted perhaps another 10,000 years. Several factors may have contributed to their demise. The Earth was warming, causing large parts of the mammoth's range to become unsuitable to it. This warming may have reduced populations to the point that they became susceptible to declines caused by human hunting, particularly since mammoths were slow-breeding animals whose young were frequently the target of human need and hunger. Regardless of the explanation, mammoths vanished thousands of years ago not only from existence, but also from prehistoric cave paintings and sculptures and, for a long time, even from human memory.

Mammoths must once have been vast in number. Their bones litter the fossil record all over the northern hemisphere and were discovered frequently in the fifteenth and sixteenth centuries during excavations for building construction. So thoroughly had the mammoth been lost to European memory that Renaissance scholars thought the exhumed skeletons were the remains of giants, a race of people wiped out by the Great Flood described in the Bible. It was not until the nineteenth century that the geneology of the mammoth was understood. But long before that, the mammoth was having a commercial impact on society because of the huge quantities of ivory it left behind, particularly in Siberia.

Siberia covers millions of square miles, and in the relatively recent past it was home to thousands of mammoths. Their tusks have survived long years in the earth and have fed the ivory trade for centuries. The Chinese were buying Siberian ivory more than 2,000 years ago, and the Mediterranean world, too, had heard by then of a place far to the north where ivory was dug from the ground. Arab traders entered the Siberian ivory business 1,000 years ago, and the English started buying mammoth ivory in the 1600s.

Throughout all of this time, no one knew the origin of the ivory. The most common theory was that the tusks were the teeth of giant, burrowing rodents that were burned up by the sun when they inadvertently reached the surface of the Earth, leaving behind only the massive teeth they used for digging. To the prescientific world, this explanation seemed much more reasonable than the idea that elephants might once have lived in the cold northern regions of the globe.

That the tusks came from elephants was proved indisputably, early in the nineteenth century, when an entire Siberian mammoth was found encased in ice along the Lena River by a wandering ivory trader. He first saw the animal as a dark shape in the ice in 1799. It was not until a warm spell in 1801 that enough ice had melted for the trader to perceive that the animal was a mammoth. When he visited the area in 1803, an unusual warm spell had melted all the ice, and the animal lay fully exposed. Word about the mammoth reached Mikhail Ivanovich Adams, a botanist in St. Petersburg, much later, and he traveled to the mammoth in

This baby mammoth died 10,000 years ago. Its body was found frozen in an excavation area in northeastern Siberia on June 23, 1977. Such finds have been made for centuries. Fossil tusks from extinct mammoths and mastodons have supplied ivory markets for thousands of years.

Siberian mammoth tusks on the ivory floor at the London docks. The tusks of at least 50,000 mammoths went through nineteenth century ivory markets, an indication of how plentiful mammoths must once have been.

1806. By then wolves and dogs had eaten some of its centuries-old flesh. Adams had the animal cut up for shipment to St. Petersburg. This was a major task, since the hide alone required ten men to lift it. Adams also had to pack the animal's hair into a separate crate, since all 37 pounds of it had fallen off when the body was moved. The Academy of Sciences in St. Petersburg bought the carcass from Adams, and it lies today in the academy museum. The fur, by the way, answered all questions about how an elephant could have survived in chill Siberia.

Knowledge about mammoths led to a mammoth fad in the United States early in the nineteenth century. Mammoth skeletons were widely displayed in traveling exhibits, and the word *mammoth* entered the common vocabulary as an adjective meaning anything large. Meanwhile, trade in mammoth ivory continued apace. A single ivory hunter brought 20,000 pounds of mammoth tusks from Siberia in one year. In the Russian town of Yakutsk, one focal point of the ivory trade, 25 tons of ivory were sold yearly during much of the 1800s. In all, the tusks of at least 50,000 mammoths reached nineteenth century markets, a fairly large number for an extinct species.

While European and Asian traders were scouring northern reaches for mammoth remains, African peoples were still dealing with living elephants, hunting them with techniques that might have been familiar to prehistoric hunters of the Northern Hemisphere. However, it is unlikely that native Africans, prior to European contact, hunted elephants with quite the dedication of northern peoples. They would have had little reason to do so, since less dangerous game was abundant. They were fully capable, however, of bringing down elephants and had devised a number of methods for doing so.

In southern and southeastern Africa, natives used *assagais*—short, iron-headed spears—in attacks upon elephants, generally impaling individual animals hundreds of times until the animals bled to death. Sometimes poisoned arrows or spears were used. One people famous for their poison was the Dorobo. They made the poison from the leaves of the *Acocantha* tree, which grew in the forests of Mount Kenya. The leaves were boiled in water for six hours, and the liquid was strained and further distilled until it became a thick, black substance that was spread on sheets of bark and stored high in trees, safely out of the reach of children. When needed the poison was applied to the tip of a short spear that would be hurled at close range at an elephant. The barbed spearhead was designed to slip off the shaft and remain in the elephant's flesh, seeping poison until the elephant died. Though death was certain, it was sometimes so slow in coming that wounded elephants were able to escape the hunter before finally dying. When a hunt was successful, though, the hunter's entire village would gather at the kill and share in the meat after carefully cutting out the poisoned flesh around the spearhead.

Another common method for killing elephants was the use of pits up to 14 feet deep and covered with branches or reeds and dried grass. The pits were dug on trails used by elephants on their way to water. Sometimes several members of a single herd might be trapped in pits and killed with spears.

During dry seasons, when grass up to 14 feet tall was highly flammable, peoples in central Africa used to ignite circles of flame around entire elephant herds. Initially a circle might be two miles in diameter, and the elephants would retreat into the circle as the flames and shouting natives drew near. The trap would tighten until eventually the elephants panicked. Explorer Samuel Baker, writing at the end of the nineteenth century, described how the elephants "at length become desperate, being maddened by fear, and panic-stricken by the wild shouts of the thousands who have surrounded them. At length, half-suffocated by the dense smoke, and terrified by the close approach of the roaring flames, the unfortunate animals charge recklessly through the fire, burnt and blinded, to be ruthlessly speared by the bloodthirsty crowd awaiting this last stampede." Natives using this method reportedly, on some occasions, killed more than a hundred elephants at once.

Another native method was the ambush. A hunter armed with a weighted spear would hide on a tree branch above an elephant trail. When an elephant passed below, the hunter would stab it with the weighted spear. The wounded elephant would rush away, the weight of the spear driving it in farther, the bashing of the spear against low tree branches tearing the wound until the animal bled to death. This method also had its automated form. A heavy iron spear weighted with a log would be attached to a wooden beam mounted over an elephant path. The beam would be rigged to cords and a wooden frame in such a way that a passing elephant would activate a trigger that would send the spear hurling down toward the animal. The device was reportedly set so that the spear, which with the log attached weighed several hundred pounds, usually struck a spot where the brain met the neck. "The blow falls like a thunder-clap," wrote nineteenth century biologist Richard Lydekker in *The New Natural History*, "and if the trap is well made, the elephant struggles and dies."

■ ELEPHANTS AND CIVILIZATION: EARLY MEETINGS

The first known mention of elephants in literature did not occur until 480 B.C. This was a report by Hanno, a Carthaginian who sought to establish settlements on the west coast of Africa, to the effect that the marshes surrounding the Tensift River near the Atlas Mountains were "haunted by elephants and multitudes of other grazing beasts."

Hanno's account was preserved only in Greek translation. It was also the Greeks who gave us our first lengthy account of the elephant. The author was Ctesias, writing roughly at the beginning of the fourth century before Christ. He described animals he saw in captivity and discussed their use in warfare. Aristotle, writing later in the fourth century, provided the first lengthy treatise on elephant biology and natural history, including a discussion of anatomy, reproduction, diet, and behavior.

At that time two types of elephant ranged throughout most of Africa south of the Sahara. The larger was the bush elephant, standing more than 8 feet tall. It lived throughout the open plains. The other variety, generally less than 8 feet tall, lived throughout the rainforests of west and west-central Africa.

The forest elephant also ranged then along the northern

A sub-adult takes a precautionary sniff to detect possible danger while feeding in Ol Turkai Arok Swamp. Swamplands have long been recognized as important elephant habitat. The earliest known account of elephants, penned by the Carthaginian explorer Hanno about 2,500 years ago, described the marshes of the Tensift River in northwest Africa as "haunted by elephants."

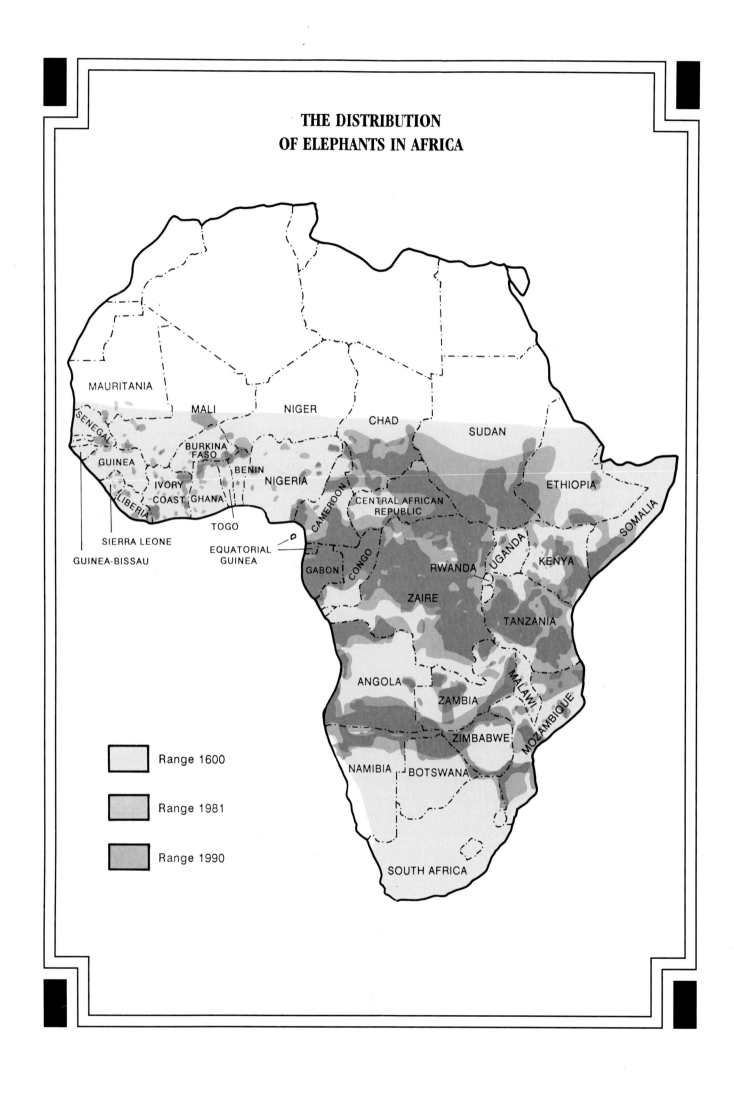

THE DISTRIBUTION
OF ELEPHANTS IN AFRICA

MAURITANIA

MALI

NIGER

CHAD

SUDAN

SENEGAL

GUINEA

BURKINA
FASO

BENIN

NIGERIA

ETHIOPIA

IVORY
COAST

GHANA

CAMEROON

CENTRAL AFRICAN
REPUBLIC

LIBERIA

TOGO

SOMALIA

SIERRA LEONE

EQUATORIAL
GUINEA

GABON

CONGO

UGANDA

KENYA

GUINEA-BISSAU

RWANDA

ZAIRE

TANZANIA

ANGOLA

MALAWI

ZAMBIA

MOZAMBIQUE

ZIMBABWE

Range 1600

NAMIBIA

BOTSWANA

Range 1981

Range 1990

SOUTH AFRICA

reaches of Ethiopia and Somalia and along northwest Africa in a region that today includes northern Morocco, northernmost Algeria, most of Tunisia, and parts of northwest Libya. Some 10,000 years earlier, the Sahara had been lush enough to feed elephants, and in that era the populations of north Africa were contiguous with those of sub-Saharan regions. The increased moisture of that time also made Egypt habitable for elephants. But the retreat of the glaciers about 10,000 years ago rendered the Sahara arid and cut the elephant's range in two. Subsequent drying trends in the last millennium before Christ made Egypt and nearby regions unsuitable for elephants.

The elephant did not become generally known to the classical world until roughly the time of Alexander the Great, in the fourth century before Christ. During the 1,000 years or so before Alexander, the Greek word *elephas* referred almost exclusively to

Cattle egrets and elephants feed in a south Kenya swamp. Egrets devour insects stirred up by elephants, an ages-old relationship of clear benefit to the birds.

The emperor Kublai, grand khan of the Mongols and Tartars, fighting from a chariot atop four elephants during a battle between Pekin and Siberia. Elephants were used as implements of war for centuries in Asia, Europe, and northern Africa.

THE EMPEROR KUBLAI.
GRAND KHAN OF THE MONGOLS AND TARTARS:
Commanding in a battle fought
between Pekin & Siberia in which were
800,000 Combatants.

ivory. Greek merchants were not even certain whether ivory, known well through trade, was animal or mineral in origin. Alexander the Great discovered its true nature when he reached India during his long journey of world conquest and found himself facing tuskers decked out in armor and trained for combat. The huge creatures were equally terrifying to the Greeks and their horses. The mere sight and smell of elephants were enough to scatter a battle line. Recognizing the elephant's potential as a war machine, Alexander acquired some elephants while in India and used them both in battle and as pack animals.

Though Alexander did not long survive his Asian battles, elephants became permanent additions to the world of the ancient Greeks as well as that of the Egyptians and Romans. In the centuries after Alexander, the elephant was used widely for warfare and for entertainment in circuses and gladiatorial games.

The Egyptian pharoahs of the third century B.C. established elephant-hunting stations along coastal Ethiopia and Somalia. They were interested partly in ivory, and ancient accounts tell how the hunters slew their prey. One method was to lie in hiding in thick forest until an elephant passed by. Then the hunter would jump upon the animal, seize its tail, and plant his feet against the elephant's left flank. Holding on with one hand as the elephant struggled to throw him off, the hunter would hack at the animal's hamstrings with a light axe until the tendons were severed and the animal fell, helpless. Then other hunters would fall upon the elephant and butcher its hindquarters, sometimes feasting on the flesh while the elephant was still alive.

Of course on occasion the elephant would crush the hunter against a tree or on the ground. This might have made an alternative method more attractive—the hunting of elephants from horseback. Apparently this was a highly serviceable technique, because its use by Arab hunters in the Sudan persisted well into the nineteenth century. Usually three or four hunters rode together, cutting a single elephant out of a herd and chasing it until, exhausted or exasperated, it turned and charged. The hunter who was the object of the charge would nimbly wheel about and gallop away, the elephant in pursuit. The other hunters were free to gallop up to the elephant from behind. When they reached it, one hunter would seize the reins of the other, who would spring to the ground and with a blow of a double-edged sword cut the elephant's hamstring.

But dead elephants were not the sole interest of the pharoahs. They also wanted live animals for battle and display. Though the native hunters of Ethiopia and Somalia refused to capture live elephants, historical accounts show that the pharoahs nevertheless acquired living pachyderms. Presumably they did this by assembling their own squadrons of hunters. Apparently the pharoahs also hired Indian elephant trainers, then as today the world's foremost elephant handlers. (In ancient Egyptian texts, the word for elephant trainer is *Indian*.)

The primary use for live elephants was warfare. Against soldiers and horses that had never encountered them, elephants were deadly. Records left by ancient Greeks and Romans indicate that a special dread visited soldiers about to meet elephants in battle.

Elephants went into war under the command of a *mahout*, the Indian name for an elephant trainer. The Romans called them *magisteri*—"masters"—or *elephantistes*. The trainers spent long years working with their elephants and had deep emotional bonds with them. During battle the trainer rode on the elephant's neck, commanding it by voice, by the pressure of his feet on the animal's ears, or by taps with the ank, or crook. Usually each elephant was escorted into battle by about 50 soldiers who protected it from the agile human enemy in much the way that fighter planes during World War II repulsed enemy attacks on cumbersome bombers.

Often the elephants were armored with bronze or iron, particularly around the head and sides. Sometimes spears or sharp irons were strapped to the elephant's tusks. The mahout also might be armed with a spear. Large baskets or roofed towers sometimes were mounted on the elephant's back so that two or three soldiers, chosen for their agility and slightness of build, could ride the elephant and shower spears and arrows on the enemy. Elephants usually fought by trampling opposing warriors and by crushing them in their trunks, though actual fighting was not the elephant's crucial role in battle. They were used primarily to cause—by their presence alone—crippling disarray and panic in enemy ranks.

Perhaps the most enduring stories about elephants in war concern the Carthaginian enemy of Rome, Hannibal. Toward the end of the third century B.C., Hannibal led an army out of Carthage, on the Bay of Tunis in North Africa, across the Mediterranean to the Iberian Peninsula. From there he cut across Europe and scaled the Alps on his way into Italy. Traveling with him was an array of war elephants. In *The War With Hannibal*, Livy described how the animals affected Roman battle lines: "After much indecisive fighting Hannibal ordered the elephants up to the front line on the chance that this might cause panic and confusion, and at first it did so: ranks and standards were thrown into turmoil; some of the men within reach were trampled to death, others broke and fled, and a section of the line was stripped bare." Describing another battle, Livy wrote: "The elephants, too, on the extreme wings caused widespread confusion, as the horses were terrified by the sight and smell of these strange beasts they had never seen before."

Unfortunately for Hannibal and anyone else who relied on elephants to turn the tide of battle, the animals worked best against inexperienced men and horses. After a little training, the soldiers found that they often could vanquish the elephants. Livy again: "The light-armed foot, specially brought in to deal with [the elephants] drove them off with their javelins, followed up, and pierced them again in the soft skin under their tails." Experience also provided means for fending off elephants. Foot soldiers and

Hannibal directing the Carthaginian army, with its caravan of elephants, across the Alps as he prepares to invade Italy to fight Rome for control of Mediterranean trade. Hannibal's use of elephants was of little avail. The Romans learned to frighten the animals, making them as dangerous to the Carthaginians as they were to the Romans.

cavalry were often armed with weapons such as scimitars and light axes that could be used to hamstring elephants. Armor bristling with iron spikes kept the elephants from using their trunks to seize warriors. Elephants could also be reduced to hopeless panic by various means, such as loud trumpet blasts or the release of squealing pigs onto the battlefield. Fire was used against elephants, including the use of flaming arrows. They also could be slowed by trenches and moveable, iron-studded barricades.

Once the elephants themselves were under assault, they often became deadly to their own soldiers, which is why the Greeks called them "common enemies." In *The War With Hannibal*, Livy tells how a Roman officer led his men "into the very thick of the turmoil caused by the solid mass of elephants and ordered them to let fly with their javelins. Every weapon found a mark—and indeed beasts of such size and packed so closely together presented no difficult target; but not all were hit, and those which had spears sticking in their backs turned and ran, like the untrustworthy creatures they are, and in their efforts to escape carried with them the others who were still untouched. . . . The poor brutes charged their own masters and caused even greater carnage amongst them than they had caused amongst the enemy—inevitably, because a frightened beast is driven more fiercely by terror than when he is under the control of his rider."

Elephants out of control could decimate their own troops and even rout their own cavalry, turning victory into defeat. But the handlers had a means for reasserting authority over panicking elephants. Livy gives an apt description: "The riders used to carry a mallet and a carpenter's chisel and when one of the creatures began to run amok and attack its own people, the keeper would put the chisel between its ears at the junction between head and neck and drive it in with a heavy blow. It was the quickest way that had been found to kill an animal of such size once it was out of control. . . ."

After battle, elephants became part of the property that victorious generals brought home for parades. The Romans also added elephants to gladitorial games. Accounts of the games have been handed down to us by writers such as Seneca and Pliny. In 55 B.C., Julius Caesar's rival, General Pompey, sponsored a memorable spectacle that apparently involved 18 elephants in a battle to the death with men armed with spears. One elephant was killed when a single spear struck it below the eye. Pliny described the desperate struggle of another elephant: "One of these animals fought in a most astonishing manner; being pierced through the feet, it dragged itself on its knees towards the troop, and seizing their bucklers, tossed them aloft into the air: and as they came to the ground they greatly amused the spectators, for they whirled round and round in the air, just as if they had been thrown up with a certain degree of skill, and not by the frantic fury of a wild beast."

At one point pandemonium threatened to ruin the whole show. Panicked elephants assaulted the iron bars that blocked the coliseum gates, throwing terror into the audience. Then, their attempt at escape futile, the elephants stood in the arena waving

their trunks in apparent desperation, trumpeting with a sound so sorrowful that they softened the hearts of those who had been amused by the spectacle of gladiators whirling through the air. Pliny wrote, "So greatly were the people affected by the scene, that forgetting the general altogether, and the munificence which had been at such pains to do them honor, the whole assembly rose up in tears, and showered curses on Pompeius. . . ."

After witnessing the spectacle, famed orator Cicero wrote, "What pleasure can it possibly be to a man of culture, when either a puny human being is mangled by a most powerful beast or a splendid beast is transfixed with a hunting spear. . . . The result was a certain compassion and a kind of feeling that the huge beast has a fellowship with the human race."

Audiences were much happier with a show some 70 years later in which a dozen elephants—dressed in flowered garments that mimicked the costumes of dancers—turned circles in the center of the arena and swayed rythmically. After sprinkling flowers on the ground, the elephants sat down to eat at a banquet table. Quite genteel at first, the animals eventually started spraying each other and their trainer with water.

In the centuries that followed, elephants were often featured in games, sometimes battling hundreds of armed men, sometimes

A bronze ingot, cast at Rome in the middle of the third century B.C., depicts an Asian elephant. Early Romans took elephants and ivory from Syria and doubtless contributed to the animal's extinction there.

Hannibal with his elephants crossing the Rhone, after a painting by Henri Motte, 1878. According to Livy the elephants were actually floated across the river on huge rafts 50 feet wide and 100 feet long, with several elephants per raft.

fighting with one group of gladiators against a second group of elephants and gladiators. In the time of the emperors Claudius and Nero, gladiators took great pride in fighting elephants one-on-one. Some elephants were trained to walk on tightropes and to take entry fees from people entering the arenas. Pliny, in a poignant tale, wrote that one circus elephant, severely beaten because it learned slowly, was found one night practicing all alone.

The elephants used in Rome and elsewhere were often captured in the wild. How the trade met the demand of the arenas is poorly understood. H.H. Scullard, in his excellent book *The Elephant in the Greek and Roman World*, suggested that the trade was controlled by the emperor and conducted by an appointee who worked directly with commercial companies. Among Roman ruins in Italy, Sicily, and North Africa are offices whose mosaic pavements and statues advertised the nature of their businesses, and a number of the artworks depict African elephants. Mosaics in private houses, too, show African elephants being loaded onto ships.

The elephant was clearly quite familiar to the ancient world, but that did not keep it from slipping into obscurity during the Dark Ages. The fall of Rome in 476 brought to a close the early history of the African elephant.

▌ AFRICA, EXPLORATION, AND ELEPHANTS

For a thousand years after the fall of Rome, the African elephant slipped from the realm of European experience. If known at all, it was only as a source of ivory. Then, in the sixteenth century,

An adult feeds on greenery while her calf suckles. Mothers usually put one front leg forward to ease access to the teat. The calf will suckle until its mother bears another calf, at which time the elder offspring will be about four and able to survive on vegetation alone.

Jumbo at home in the London Zoo, prior to his sale to circus-owner P. T. Barnum. Jumbo was revered in England, where he became something of a national pet during his stay at the zoo.

Europeans started to colonize the African coast, and the African elephant soon reappeared in Europe. From 1665 to 1681, an elephant from the Congo was kept in the Versailles bestiary, where it apparently became an assimilated Frenchman—it received a daily ration of at least 3 gallons of wine and was reportedly fed pails of soup into which it would dip bread as might a human diner.

From this time forward, African elephants made increasingly frequent appearances in European zoos and circuses. Perhaps the most famous African elephant of all time lived out his life in the nineteenth century. He was still young when he arrived in the London Zoo on June 26, 1865. Sent by the Jardin des Plantes de Paris in exchange for an Indian rhinoceros, he stood 5 feet 6 inches tall, and his name was Jumbo. He was soon a zoological celebrity, eating with gusto the myriad buns offered by the public and carrying children on his back.

But Jumbo's career as an amusement park vehicle came to an abrupt end in 1881 when, as a mature bull standing 11 feet tall, he became untrustworthy. In a letter to the London Zoological Society Council, the zoo superintendent wrote of Jumbo on December 14, 1881, that he had "no doubt whatever that the animal's condition has at times been such that he would kill anyone (except Scott [Jumbo's keeper]) who would venture alone into his den, but up to the present time Scott has had, and still has, the animal perfectly and completely under his control. . . . in the event of illness or accident to the keeper (Scott) I fear I should have to ask permission to destroy the animal, as no other keeper would undertake the management of this fine but dangerous beast."

As a result of Jumbo's aggressiveness, the zoo decided to sell him to P.T. Barnum, the American circus magnate and showman, for 2,000 pounds. But this was not the sale of just any zoo animal. Barnum was buying Jumbo, and Jumbo was something of a national institution. He was revered almost as highly as the monarchy itself and even inspired an array of songs and marches. When

Jumbo is hauled from the Battery to Madison Square Garden in New York City, April 19, 1882. Despite tremendous public opposition, Jumbo had been sold by the London Zoo to P. T. Barnum because, zoo officials believed, the elephant had become dangerous.

the sale was announced in the newspapers in January 1882, it precipitated a headlong rush by public and press to keep Jumbo out of Barnum's hands. A court injunction temporarily stopped the sale, and newspapers and school children mounted a campaign to keep Jumbo in England. They even appealed to Barnum himself, but to no avail. Barnum wrote to the editor of the *Daily Telegraph* "and the British nation" that a "hundred thousand pounds would be no inducement to cancel the purchase. . . ."

Jumbo was lured into a large wooden crate in March 1882 and hauled out of the zoo on a horse-drawn wagon. Jumbo wasted little time in easing his trunk through the slats of his crate and pulling some hairs from the tail of one of the horses. This caused the entire team to bolt, but the driver—presumably helped by the immense weight of the load—was able to get the horses under control without disaster.

Jumbo sailed from England on March 25 and arrived in the United States on April 9. In the United States, he lost his aggressive temper and became quite tractable. Sylvia Sikes, in her book *The Natural History of the African Elephant*, speculated that Jumbo's agressiveness may have stemmed from the growth of his fifth molar. The massive molars with which African elephants grind their food grow one after another over a period of years, the new tooth moving in from the rear and pushing out the older tooth in front. In 1881 Jumbo was about 20 years old, the age at which elephants cut their fifth molar. By the time he got to the United States, the molar may have been in place, accounting for the sudden moderation of his temper. The sixth molar would not have appeared for about 25 years more, so Jumbo should have been placid for a long time, making P.T. Barnum's investment in him quite sound.

But in the end Barnum did not get full value out of Jumbo. In mid-September 1885, after the final show scheduled for St. Thomas, Ontario, a keeper led Jumbo and another elephant named Tom along a railroad track to their cars in the circus train. The keeper had been assured that no trains were due for at least an hour on the track he was following, so he was completely surprised when the headlight of a locomotive cut into view a mere 500 yards from him, Jumbo, and Tom. The elephants fled down the track as the engineer tried to stop, but to no avail. The train was on a downhill grade and within moments slammed into Tom, throwing him into a ditch. Jumbo was then struck in the hindlegs. He roared, turned, and fell, and the first car struck his back as the engine and two cars were derailed. Within 15 minutes, Jumbo died of his wounds. His mounted body was subsequently dis-

In dawn mist, elephants move to their feeding grounds, appearing as huge, silent shadows. In deep fog the animals rely on sound and smell to avoid being separated.

played at Tufts University in Boston, and in the late 1880s was sent to England for a tour. It was destroyed in a fire at Tufts in 1973.

If, by the nineteenth century, the civilized world had not been reaching deeply into Africa, Jumbo might have died beneath the wide-crowned trees of some distant savannah, the roar of lions or the trumpeting of his own kind fading in his ears. Jumbo's death on an Ontario railroad track is therefore strangely symbolic of the extent to which Victorian society was delving into the Dark Continent and carrying its treasures away.

SAFARI:
ON THE TRACK
OF ADVENTURE

Nothing but breathing the air of Africa, and actually walking through it, can communicate the indescribable sensations which every traveller of feeling will experience.

William J. Burchell, *Travels in the Interior of Southern Africa*, 1824

∎

In going back to that country, my object is to open up traffic along the banks of the Zambesi, and also to preach the Gospel. . . . By encouraging the native propensity for trade, the advantages that might be derived in a commercial point of view are incalculable; nor should we lose sight of the inestimable blessings it is in our power to bestow upon the unenlightened African, by giving him the light of Christianity. Those two pioneers of civilization—Christianity and commerce— should ever be inseparable.

David Livingstone, in a lecture at Cambridge University, December 1857

∎

Again and again, in the continents new to peoples of European stock, we have seen the spectacle of a high civilization all at once thrust into and superimposed upon a wilderness of savage men and savage beasts. Nowhere, and at no time, has the contrast been more strange and striking than in British East Africa during the last dozen years.

Theodore Roosevelt, *African Game Trails*, 1910

∎

We could not, unfortunately, relive *African Game Trails* entirely. We will have no memories of the laden caravan nor of the lion's charge; a land-rover is neither as romantic nor as companionable as a horse; and there is too little left, even in East Africa, that is "unworn of man."

Kermit Roosevelt, *A Sentimental Safari: An Account of a Safari Made by Kermit Roosevelt and His Two Sons to the Same "African Game Trails" First Visited by His Famous Grandfather, President Theodore Roosevelt, Fifty Years Before*, 1960

∎

A continent ages quickly once we come to it.

Ernest Hemingway, *Green Hills of Africa*, 1935

∎

ALTHOUGH GREEK AND ROMAN SHIPS REACHED northern Africa many centuries before Christ, Africa south of the Sahara remained long beyond the reach of European sail. It was not until the final years of the fifteenth century that a Portuguese ship under the command of Vasco da Gama rounded the Cape of Good Hope and became the first European vessel to reach the Indian Ocean via Africa.

In the sixteenth century, Portugal took the lead in world trade and established several coastal colonies along African shores. The Portuguese even rivaled the Arabs in trying to control trade in eastern Africa, a region the Arabs had entered 500 years before. But despite this European presence, the African interior remained nearly unscathed by European contact for three centuries after the first Portuguese coastal settlements were established. This was largely the result of financial concerns. The scramble for colonies and trade that made Europe so politically volatile in the sixteenth and seventeenth centuries resulted in overextended government budgets and military forces. To avoid further expense, the imperialist nations actively discouraged settlement in the African interior.

Nevertheless, some settlement did reach beyond the coasts. The Dutch settlers who started coming to southern Africa in the 1650s—and who succeeded in wiping out the area's lions, hippos, and elephants within the next 70 years—thwarted their government's plan for containment by wandering north into the interior in the early eighteenth century. But these few settlers were not part of a concerted effort to colonize new lands. They tended to remain beyond government control and protection, fighting without official assistance against the Africans upon whose land they encroached. Consequently, when the nineteenth century dawned, Africa beyond the fringe of its coasts was still *terra incognita*. But the pressures of history were mounting, and Africa could not hope to escape them.

An elephant flaps and feeds among palms and fallen acacia trees in Amboseli's Ol Turkai Swamp.

∎ EARLY SAFARIS: A NEW ERA

In 1806 Napoleon was battling all across Europe, and France and Holland were at war with the British. That year England sent 63 warships and some 6,000 soldiers into southern Africa and, in an effort to ensure British domination of the seas, took over the strategically important cape colonies of the Dutch East India Company. England did not relinquish the colonies for nearly a century.

Once firmly in control of South Africa, the British adopted the Dutch policy of discouraging travel and colonization north of the Orange River. This was in part Britain's effort to keep an unoccupied buffer between the settled lands and the militarily powerful Bantu peoples. The policy was also meant to limit the

Placid scenes such as this, in a Kenyan swamp, must often have greeted Africa's first European explorers. Africa is one of the few places where visitors can still sense what the world must have been like before humans dominated the globe.

crown's responsibility for defending the interior. Consequently, in the early years of the nineteenth century the dominant European influence in the interior tended to be missionaries who went to preach to the natives, along with a scattering of renagade farmers and livestockmen and an occasional ivory hunter or explorer.

This began to change in 1808, thanks to the fickleness of a young English girl named Lucia Green. In that year Lucia Green set sail from Fulham to meet her fiance, botanist William Burchell, on a southern Atlantic island called St. Helena (the same St. Helena where Napoleon would spend his last years). It was a long voyage, and Lucia Green was a young girl, and the captain of the vessel on which she sailed cut a dashing figure. By the time the ship reached St. Helena, the captain had won Lucia Green's heart; Burchell was left in the lurch.

In his sorrow Burchell resigned as botanist for the East India Company and, stimulated by stories told by African travelers, in 1810 made his way to Cape Town, on the continent's southern tip. It was the perfect place for a botanist and former junior gardener at the Royal Botanic Gardens in Kew. On a single square mile of mountain slopes outside of Cape Town, Burchell collected more than 200 plant species and concluded that this was the richest botanical site he had ever encountered. He quickly embarked on a plan to journey far into the interior, deeper than any European had gone before.

It took Burchell six months to plan and supply the trip. He had to get formal permission from the governor, build a wagon to carry his gear, hire a staff of Africans, purchase the oxen that would haul his wagon at a maximum speed of 3 miles an hour, and secure all the tools of his trade. Finally, on June 19, 1811, this man who had never spent a single night in the outdoors headed into the unknown reaches of southern Africa, a land where he could expect to encounter not only dangerous animals but also hostile native peoples. Both the place and its wildlife were so little known that even Burchell, with his scientific background, could seriously hope to finance his trip by bringing back to England and offering for sale (at a price of 7,500 pounds) the remains of an animal he fully anticipated collecting—a unicorn.

For four years Burchell wandered with his cadre of ten Hottentots—a native people long oppressed by the Dutch—across some 4,500 miles of southern Africa, raising the British flag every Sunday morning wherever he was camped. He became resourceful, independent, and ever busy. He learned to use rhinoceros blood, vegetable juice, and earth for making the ink and paints he

used in some 500 botanical drawings. He made candles from sheep fat, worked on a dictionary of the native language, collected 40,000 plant specimens, and measured the distance he traveled each day by using a formula based on the amount of ground covered by each revolution of his wagon's wheels. He created a map of the regions he explored—a *magnum opus* of a map that measured over 8 feet long and nearly 8 feet high. He learned to eat hippo meat and to relish the flesh of the eland, an antelope that grows to 6 feet at the shoulder and weighs up to 1,500 pounds. He occasionally functioned as a doctor, as when treating a Hottentot who blew off most of one hand when a gun misfired. Burchell became the first European to report the existence of the white rhino and the quagga, a zebra-like animal that would be hunted to extinction by 1883. He came to respect his Hottentot

A wary warthog pauses from his rooting duties to suspiciously eye an intruder.

A crowned crane duo scouts the grasses for insects and seeds.

staff, to admire or dislike them as individuals, rather than to treat them as the inferiors that Dutch law declared "shall for life be the lawful property of such burghers as may possess them, and serve in bondage from generation to generation."

Though he did not know it, when he returned to Cape Town Burchell had completed the first true safari. This East African Swahili word for trip or journey—derived from the Arabic noun *safariya*, which means much the same thing—would not become part of the common vocabulary until late in the nineteenth century. Nevertheless Burchell had established a special pattern of African travel, a pattern that would be duplicated by many others in the decades ahead.

Perhaps the earliest of Burchell's imitators was a young man from Kent who sailed for Bombay as a 16-year-old second lieutenant in the East India Company's corps of engineers. His name was Cornwallis Harris, and he had a lifelong interest in hunting. While in India he read Burchell's published accounts of the long trip and was mesmerized by the rich array of wildlife that Africa offered the hunter. He was particularly enchanted with the idea of killing a giraffe. He even dreamt of giraffes, and his hunts in India only served to intensify his desire to shoot in Africa.

In 1836 Harris fell ill with an Indian fever. The disease was a tremendous stroke of good luck, because Harris, as an essential part of his medical treatment, was ordered to spend two years of convalescence in southern Africa. Harris quickly followed his own imaginative interpretation of this order. Soon after his arrival in Africa, he and William Richardson, a friend from the Bombay Civil Service, trekked off into the wilderness in the company of eight Hottentots, 42 oxen, and 12 horses. Their two wagons were packed with brandy, dried fish, cheese, coffee, tea, and some items that Burchell might have found unnecessary—bullet molds and lead ingots as well as 18,000 ready-to-fire bullets. Despite these accoutrements the safari began less than auspiciously. The Hottentot staff, most of them ex-convicts, were drunk at the time of embarkation and had to be loaded like firewood into the wagons. One Hottentot, sober enough to drive a wagon, was nevertheless drunk enough to ram it into a house as the troupe left the town of Graaf-Reinet.

The areas through which Harris first passed were not the untouched lands that Burchell had seen nearly 30 years before. Though various antelope species abounded, some had been ruined by hunting. Blesbok and hartebeest, two types of antelope, had been reduced to a single herd each. The hippopotamus, rhi-

A mounted horseman rushes after game on the vast, virtually unexplored plains of Meritsane, South Africa. This 1841 watercolor was painted by William Cornwallis, one of the first Europeans to go on a hunting safari in Africa.

The red-billed oxpecker feeds on ticks and other parasites, doing the African buffalo an important and comforting service.

noceros, eland, and elephant were dwindling in the lands south of the Orange River. Even the Bushman were no longer the masters of their domain. Literally hunted like animals both by the native Bantu and by the Boers, as Dutch settlers were called, the Bushmen had been reduced to poverty, starvation, and constant flight.

Eventually Harris and Richardson came to the lands where big, dangerous game still survived. But before they could hunt, they had one more obstacle to overcome. This was Mzilikazi, headman of the Matabele, a clan of Zulu. Mzilikazi was a warrior king who had an iron grip on the lands that the Englishmen wanted to hunt. His thousands of warriors were busy consolidating their leader's power, raiding other native peoples, killing all their men, and seizing their women and property. His rapacity depopulated vast areas, leaving hundreds of miles of countryside devoid of people.

Missionaries and even Hottentots told Harris and Richardson to avoid Mzilikazi, but the duo was determined to hunt in Matabele land, their determination inspired particularly by reports of the elephant herds roamed there. They insisted upon meeting Mzilikazi, and, with the good luck that seemed ever to badger Harris, they proved able to purchase Mzilikazi's friendship with generous applications of red beads, mirrors, copper wire, Irish snuff, and various garments ranging from suspenders to shoes. Harris even managed to give the Zulu king a Persian carpet. Placated, Mzilikazi gave the hunters free entry into the hunting grounds.

In the land of the Matabele, Harris and Richardson found the Africa of their hearts' desires. Rushing across the plains on horseback, they fired upon giraffe and rhino and gunned down eland and waterbuck, the latter a large antelope weighing about a quarter of a ton. Then, nearing the Magaliesberg Mountains, they found signs of elephants and followed the animals' trail. Along the way they hunted and fed upon cape buffalo and found rhino so numerous that they once counted 22 within half a mile. They saw no elephants, however, until November 7, 1836, when Harris followed an elephant trail along the Sant River and entered a valley in which, as he wrote, the "whole face of the landscape was ac-

William Cornwallis, like many explorers of his day, took upon himself the task of cataloging, by illustration, the animals he saw. This is his 1841 watercolor of a sassaby and a hartebeest, two species of antelope.

Elephants feeding in the Amboseli bush are dwarfed by Mt. Kilimanjaro. The 19,340-foot-high mountain, the highest on the continent, has been an almost fabled landmark since the earliest days of eastern African exploration.

Tanzania's Mt. Kilimanjaro, just across the Kenyan border, dominates the Amboseli landscape to the south. Hemingway introduced the landmark to millions of readers in his short story, "The Snows of Kilimanjaro," and Queen Victoria is said to have given it as a gift to a cousin before she ever saw the majestic peak.

A mother and offspring, accompanied by an aunt, sister, or other family member, feed in Ol Turkai Arok Swamp in Amboseli National Park. This scenario would have made early hunter Cornwallis Harris's trigger finger itch. Yet even he was moved by the apparent sorrow of a baby elephant he had orphaned.

tually covered with wild elephants. There could not have been fewer than 300 within the scope of our vision."

Never a willing practitioner of quiet observation, Harris immediately dispatched a contingent of men to drive the elephants toward him and Richardson. As the animals moved up the valley, the hunters blasted away. Many elephants were killed in what appears to have been an unleashing of wanton bloodlust. The slaughter was so vast that even Harris was saddened, particularly after he recalled, with seemingly uncharacteristic sentimentality, a favorite trained elephant from whose back he had potted tigers while in India. When a baby elephant that he had orphaned mourned beside its fallen mother and wrapped its trunk around Harris's leg, the hunter felt compelled to adopt the animal. He tried to feed it, but it soon died.

Harris and Richardson were nearing the end of their hunt. But before it came to a close, Harris killed his giraffe, a big bull that he chased on horseback and shot 17 times before it died. As he turned back toward the south, Harris also shot a sable antelope, a large, black animal with long, scimitar horns that is perhaps the most beautiful of all antelope. It was the first sable antelope encountered by a European, and Harris had the honor of introducing it to science. The discovery of a new species fulfilled a dream that to Harris was second in importance only to slaying giraffes. As Harris himself put it, "Next to the slaughter of the proud giraffe, the desire nearest to my heart was to discover something new. . . . some stately quarry unknown to science and adorning no museum saving mine own." Thus Harris's luck persisted.

The hunt finally came to an end when Harris and Richardson reached Graaff-Reinet on January 24, 1837. Harris later published accounts of his trip, including a folio of 31 colored engravings in the tradition of such wildlife artists as Alexander Wilson and John James Audubon. He returned to India, later made an official expedition to the area now called Ethiopia, and in 1848, back in India, fell ill with fever and died at 41.

One regret that Harris expressed about his African sojourn was that he had not brought along a third wagon. Lack of an extra wagon had made it necessary for him to leave a number of elephant tusks behind. Future African hunters would not make this mistake, since many of them were compelled to hunt primarily for ivory and the profits it offered. Harris opened the way for such men, turning southern Africa into the gateway to the interior. But other explorers were opening other parts of Africa. Among them was the missionary David Livingstone, who found the southern reaches too infested with missionaries to suit his tastes and turned instead to east Africa. The travel accounts penned by Livingstone and Harris combined into an irresistible lure for European adventurers. By the end of the nineteenth century, the word *safari* had become part of the vocabulary, and *white hunter* connoted a profession.

▮ ELEPHANT HUNTERS

The men who pursued Africa's game trails were an unusual breed. They often were isolated for months in the wilderness, traveling in company of native peoples, removed for seemingly endless days from the comforts, both social and physical, that their own world would have bestowed upon them. The histories of these men show some important common threads. They tended to be avid hunters from childhood, more comfortable with open skies and wide horizons than drawing rooms. They often were impatient with schooling and unhappy with social restrictions. In the African bush, they could make their own rules, and in the isolation and danger of their lives they found happiness and contentment.

One hunter, James Sutherland, probably spoke for all when he wrote of the attraction the African bush held for the young adventurers: "To all intents and purposes we are absolutely free; there is no vexatious etiquette to be observed; I can burst into a hearty laugh without shocking the ridiculous propriety of a crowded street; I do not require to wear this kind of waistcoat or that kind of tie. The morning coat and silk hat I wore on my last brief visit to England, I flung into the sea in sheer exuberance of spirits, when I left Marseilles glad to be quit of costly insanity—even a bowler hat is a ludicrous menace to my sense of natural comfort. . . . There is also something wistful, tender and infinitely beautiful that forms an undercurrent to the magnificent heedlessness of the wild. It calls and calls."

One who answered that call early was Gordon Cumming, born in Scotland and educated at Eton. By the time he was 11 years old, he had built an impressive collection of hunting trophies from northern Scotland. At 19 he was in India as a soldier, and four years later, in 1843, he was in southern Africa with the Cape Mounted Rifles. There he resigned from service and went hunting for roughly the next five years.

Cumming loved elephant hunting, perhaps because, given the shooting capacity of his armaments, the hunts usually turned into pitched battles during which he and a wounded elephant alter-

nately chased one another for hours. Cumming often shot at elephants only 40 or 50 feet away and required up to three dozen shots to finish one. A sort of savannah gourmet, Cumming favored baked elephant feet and trunk. Sometimes his feeding habits were merely expedient. Once, in a hunt described in Bartle Bull's fascinating book, *Safari: A Chronicle of Adventure*, "hot and thirsty from a long chase after a female oryx, the most exhausting antelope for a horse to run down, Cumming finally shot her, and then sprang from the saddle as she fell and drank the warm milk from her teats."

Cumming's exploits made him a celebrity when, after his return to England in 1848, he wrote two popular books about his hunting years. In addition to fame, he and many like him made fortunes by focusing on elephant hunting and the ivory trade. Sport and business became synonymous. One famous elephant hunter reportedly shot a thousand elephants in 40 years of hunting. Livingstone estimated that 30,000 elephants were killed yearly from the 1840s to the 1870s to supply the ivory trade.

Elephant hunting was a dreadfully dangerous undertaking for a nineteenth century hunter. The weapons used during most of the century were cumbersome and not particularly effective. A single-shot firearm might weigh nearly 20 pounds, and though it might fire a bullet that weighed up to a quarter pound, the bullets lacked the knock-down or shocking power of today's rifles, which can drop an elephant or rhino in its tracks. Moreover, the hunters often were forced to cast their own bullets. Unless the lead that was the main component was mixed with tin or mercury, the bullet tended to disintegrate as it plowed into a large animal.

To kill an elephant with a single shot, even with a hardened bullet, a hunter would have had to get within 50 yards and fire directly into the brain. Consequently the hunts regularly turned into dangerous affairs for hunters and into lingering, painful deaths for quarry. It was not unusual for hunters to shoot a rhino or elephant a half dozen or a dozen times before felling it. Harris reported one rhino that took 27 shots, and an elephant that took 50.

The slow death of a wounded elephant gave the animal plenty of time for defense. Frederick Selous, who arrived in Africa in the 1870s and lived long enough to die from a German bullet during World War I, described an incident in which an elephant he had wounded turned on him. He had hunted the elephant on horseback, and his horse was too tired to avoid the elephant's charge. His description of what must have seemed a nightmare come to life, with the horse moving languidly as the elephant crashed

(OPPOSITE)
Night arrives in a fire-red sky at Amboseli National Park as a marabou stork settles down in the withered branches of a dead acacia tree. The splendor of wild Africa had irresistible charm for early hunters and explorers. One of them wrote, "There is a fascination to me in the remembrance of the past in all its connections: the free life, the self-dependence, the boring into what was then a new country . . . and were I not a married man with children and grandchildren, I believe I should head back to Africa again, and end my days in the open air. . . ."

A bull elephant takes a break from feeding on the acacia tree he knocked down before sunrise.
He is in musth, the male breeding season, so his aggression levels are running high. This is the sort
of target that old-time hunter Gordon Cumming sought out for a running battle, during which
Cumming would alternately shoot at and flee from the elephant.

down upon Selous, is told with singularly understated emotion: "Digging my spurs into my horse's ribs, I did my best to get him away, but he was so thoroughly done that, instead of springing forwards, which was what the emergency required, he only started at a walk, and was just breaking into a canter when the elephant was upon us. I heard two short sharp screams above my head, and had just time to think it was all over with me, when, horse and all, I was dashed to the ground. For a few seconds I was half stunned by the violence of the shock, and the first thing I became aware of was a very strong smell of elephant."

The smell was strong because Selous, apparently too stunned to know it, was being crushed under the elephant's chest. He discovered this soon after he became aware of the smell: "At the

Head up, ears out, eyes wide, this young bull makes his warning clear before vigorously shaking his head. The massive skulls of these animals made it difficult for early hunters to kill them cleanly. Some hunters needed 50 shots to bring down an elephant. The activity was dangerous for hunters and ultimately fatal to elephant populations, which quickly succumbed to heavy hunting in the early years of Africa's invasion by Europeans.

At the first hint of danger, family members form a wall around a week-old calf, the most vulnerable member of the group. This reaction demonstrates the advantages of strong family bonds. However, such a defensive response also makes the animals extremely vulnerable to poachers and is even used against them during official cull operations.

same instant I felt that I was still unhurt, and that, though in an unpleasant predicament, I had still a chance of life. I was, however, pressed down on the ground in such a way that I could not extricate my head. At last, with a violent effort, I wrenched myself loose, and threw my body over sideways so that I could rest on my hands. As I did so I saw the hind-legs of the elephant standing like two pillars before me."

For the first time, Selous realized what was going on. The enraged elephant was on top of him: "She was on her knees, with her head and tusks in the ground, and I had been pressed down under her chest, but luckily behind her fore-legs. Dragging myself from under her, I regained my feet, and made a hasty retreat, having had rather more than enough of elephants for the time being."

He must have gotten over it, though, because he went on to kill many more elephants for their ivory.

Some nineteenth century hunters were troubled by the agonized deaths to which they were subjecting Africa's big game and sought to dispatch animals quickly. One of these rare individuals was William Cotton Oswell, who roamed Africa for nearly a decade, beginning in 1844. He developed a special technique for getting close enough to an elephant to kill it quickly and cleanly. On horseback he would ride up close to an elephant herd and pick a single animal for constant harassment. Oswell's goal was to separate the animal from the herd, generally by getting it to charge him or to flee ahead of the herd. Oswell wrote, "in either case you have gained your object—separation. If he charges, put the horse to a gallop and let him follow you, the further the better. Watch as he slacks off, keeping about twenty yards ahead, and pull up sharp when he comes to stand. He is too blown to charge again, and when he turns to go after his mates he must give you his side; one or two shots carefully placed at short range are enough, and you are away again after the flying herd. The oftener you attack the easier the victory, for the heavy beasts get tired, and in consequence are much less difficult to kill."

Hunters such as Selous made reputations for themselves, and as their fame spread they were hired as hunting guides by visitors to Africa. The rise of the white hunter late in the nineteenth century shows clearly how much Africa was changing. From a land officially barred, if at all possible, to settlers, it became increasingly a place in which European and American hunters could pursue their dreams and fantasies of living and shooting in a pristine, virtually prehistoric world. The interior was no longer off limits, a policy change brought about by four developments.

One of these was the invention of the steamboat, which eased travel to Africa. Another was the opening of the Suez canal, which shortened the trip to east Africa. The third was the discovery that quinine could be used against malaria, a disease that shortened the lives of many early African explorers. And, finally, the interior was made accessible by the invention of the machine gun. Until the rapid-fire machine gun was invented, the effectively hostile native peoples defended the interior with stunning success, except in those rare confrontations in which European forces outnumbered them. With the machine gun, British, French, German, and other troops could mow down any Africans who displayed aggressive disenchantment with European enlightenment. Thus, by the end of the nineteenth century, railroads were penetrating the

A large bull elephant and African buffalo feed peacefully together in the high grass of Enkongo Narok Swamp. Pursuit of beasts such as these drew early hunters deep into Africa and helped open the continent to settlement.

interior of Africa, particularly in the east, and the age of the tourist/hunter had begun.

For many early white hunters, the changes that European contact brought to Africa were a source of sadness and regret. William Cotton Oswell, writing in his old age, gave voice to this melancholy: "There is a fascination to me in the remembrance of the past in all its connections: the free life, the self-dependence, the boring into what was then a new country; the feeling as you lay under your canvas that you were looking at the stars from a point on the earth whence no other European had ever seen them; the hope that every patch of bush, every little rise, was the only thing between you and some strange sight or scene—these are with me still; and were I not a married man with children and grandchildren, I believe I should head back to Africa again, and end my days in the open air. . . . But I am writing of close upon fifty years ago. Africa is nearly used up; she belongs no more to the Africans and the beasts; Boers, gold-seekers, diamond-miners and experimental farmers—all of them (from my point of view) mistakes—have changed the face of her. A man must be a first-rate sportsman now to keep himself and his family; houses stand where we once shot elephants, and the railway train will soon be whistling and screaming through all hunting-fields south of the Zambesi."

Africa's new game trails, a by-product of burgeoning tourism. Roads are churned into mud-clogged streams by tour-bus traffic in Amboseli National Park when the rainy season arrives a month earlier than usual. Kenya roads often become impassable after days of rain, even for 4-wheel-drive vehicles.

▌ AFRICAN GAME TRAILS

During the opening decades of the twentieth century, Africa became accustomed to the tread of the gentleman hunter. Perhaps first and foremost among the new breed was Theodore Roosevelt,

who with his son Kermit went to Africa in 1909, shortly after his second presidential term ended. One of his assistants for the hunt was Frederick Selous nearly 40 years before. He had come to Africa to hunt elephants for a living. Once in 1878 he and two companions killed 22 elephants and took 700 pounds of ivory in a single day. Selous planned Roosevelt's safari, setting the precedent for the white hunter business of the ensuing decades.

Roosevelt's trip took him from Nairobi, Kenya, across Lake Victoria to Uganda and up through the Sudan. He began the trip into what he called "game country" on one of the railroads against which Oswell's lament might have been directed. In typical Teddy style, he rode not in the train, but on a seat built for him on the cowcatcher. So it was from the cowcatcher that Roosevelt got his first glimpse of game country. He wrote in *African Game Trails*, his account of the trip, that "it was literally like passing through a vast zoological garden. . . . At one time we passed a herd of a dozen or so great giraffes, cows and calves, cantering along through the open woods. . . . Again, still closer, four waterbuck cows, their big ears thrown forward, stared at us without moving until we passed. Hartebeests were everywhere; one herd was on the track, and when the engine whistled they bucked and sprang with ungainly agility and galloped clear of the danger. . . . Huge black ostriches appeared from time to time. Once a troop of impalla, close by the track, took fright; and as the beautiful creatures fled we saw now one and now another bound clear over the high bushes. A herd of zebra clattered across a cutting of the line not a hundred yards ahead of the train. . . . "

Roosevelt had come to hunt. He wrote in his book, "Game butchery is as objectionable as any other form of wanton cruelty or barbarity; but to protest against all hunting of game is a sign of softness of head, not of soundness of heart." He proceeded to hunt with gusto, seeking "desired specimens of both sexes of all the species of big game that Kermit and I could shoot, as well as complete series of all the smaller mammals." Though the amount of wildlife that the Roosevelt party killed drew harsh criticism from the press, Roosevelt believed himself justified because he was collecting specimens for museum display. He and Kermit shot 512 animals, including 17 lions, three leopards, seven cheetahs, 20 rhinos, eight hippos, 10 eland, 10 buffalo, 10 zebras, 10 giraffes, and a large number of various antelope and birds. "Kermit and I kept about a dozen trophies for ourselves;" he wrote, "otherwise we shot nothing that was not used either as a museum specimen or for meat—usually for both purposes. . . . we did not

A young adult appears to be resting, giving its trunk a break from grass-tugging.

Theodore Roosevelt and a bull elephant shot during his 1910 tour of Africa. In many ways Roosevelt's trip marked the beginning of the safari era and the ascendance of the white hunter in colonial Africa. Even at that early date, railroads were starting to penetrate the continent, opening Africa to the modern world.

kill a tenth, nor a hundredth part of what we might have killed had we been willing."

Among the tally were 11 elephants. He killed his first with only two shots, then tracked in vain for an elephant one of his party had wounded. Fearing that the hide of the first elephant would quickly become unsuitable for preservation, Roosevelt and his companions abandoned the search for the wounded animal. "So back we turned to where the dead tusker lay," he wrote, "and I felt proud indeed as I stood by the immense bulk of the slain monster and put my hand on the ivory. The tusks weighed a hundred and thirty pounds the pair." The death of the elephant created the opportunity for Roosevelt to discover the epicurean delight he would recall most fondly from his time in Africa, elephant-trunk soup.

Roosevelt's safari, funded in part by Andrew Carnegie and

costing the equivalent of a million dollars today, set the scene for the safaris that followed, with khaki-clad hunters in pith helmets converging on Africa from distant parts of the globe and following professional white hunters in pursuit of game.

Kenya, called British East Africa in Roosevelt's time, became one of the most popular hunting places. Barely 25 years after Roosevelt, another famous American came to Kenya on safari. This was Ernest Hemingway, who with his wife Pauline and friend Charles Thompson hunted from November 1933 to February 1934, bagging four lions, two leopards, a variety of antelope, a rhino, and 35 hyenas.

Apparently mastered by his own competitive spirit, Hemingway turned the hunt into an uncomfortable contest between himself and Thompson. He became alternately morose and boastful as Thompson persistently bested the size of Hemingway's trophies. When Thompson, in the final days of the hunt, killed a kudu antelope with horns larger than those of one shot by Hemingway, Hemingway seemed to make an adjustment. When he went to bed, he wrote in *Green Hills of Africa*, "I was bitter and I was bitter all night long. In the morning, though, it was gone. It was all gone and I have never had it again."

Phillip Percival, Hemingway's guide and one of the old Africa hands who had accompanied Theodore Roosevelt during part of his safari, told the writer, "We have very primitive emotions. . . . It's impossible not to be competitive. Spoils everything, though."

Apparently it did not spoil everything for Hemingway. Years afterward he said, "I love Africa, and I find it's another home, and anytime a man can feel that, not counting where he's born, is where he's meant to go." In 1953 he went back to Africa with his fourth wife, Mary, and hunted again with Percival. By then, Africa was greatly changed from the world of Burchell and Harris, or even from that of Selous and the young Percival. The bush travelers were no longer vigorous and eccentric explorers in search of adventure, and the land was increasingly less wild and untouched.

Kermit Roosevelt, Jr., Theodore Roosevelt's grandson, demonstrated this in 1960, when he and his son followed in the African footsteps of Theodore Roosevelt and Kermit Sr. He found that much of the wildlands had been transformed into breeding grounds for livestock and that overgrazing by cattle was turning once fertile, game-crowded savannahs into desolate wastes. The big game herds, he wrote in *A Sentimental Safari*, "are diminishing each year, and at a dangerous rate. Already in Kenya, lions and rhinos are dangerously depleted; so are cheetah, wild dog, caracol (lynx), roan antelope, and sable. Sable are practically extinct;

Cattle grazing on Tsavo National Park borders are causing serious erosion problems because they destroy vegetative cover that normally slows the flow of rain water. The damage is most apparent from the air, where cattle-grazed areas show up as extensive stretches of bare, red earth with dispersed patches of grass. Under natural conditions, red patches are spots on a vast green plain.

only a hundred or so are left, in a small area on the coast. The more common game are also slowly diminishing in number—kongoni and wildebeest, Grant's and Thompson's gazelles, zebra, etc."

Africa was the Dark Continent no more.

Kermit Roosevelt's safari occurred on a cusp of great change in Africa. The colonial era was shuddering to a halt. By the end of the decade, many of the colonial governments that had controlled African politics for centuries passed into history. By the early 1970s, the new African governments were reassessing the role of the hunting safari. In 1973 Tanzania banned hunting. In 1977 Kenya, the capital of the safari world, closed its borders to hunting. Bans followed in other nations. At the same time, political turmoil in nations such as Sudan and Uganda made hunting in other regions untenable.

Hunting is still permitted in several African nations. But for others, such as Kenya, the hunting ban is a symbol of the new Africa. Apparently the ban has not affected the eagerness of visitors to travel in Africa. Tourism is Kenya's biggest source of foreign revenue. Parks are crowded with visitors armed not with guns but with cameras. They travel the bush in buses, and they

Cattle graze on the Tsavo West National Park border near Lake Jipe. They sometimes wander onto park property, competing with wildlife for fodder and causing erosion by stripping the ground bare of grass.

Tour buses bunch together, forming an elephant jam. The average watching time per stop is around two minutes. During that time the driver may not bother to cut his engine. Nearly 80 percent of a wildlife drive is spent moving from animal to animal. The average park visit is two days.

do not linger for weeks or months as the hunters did, but rather race along briskly. The average time a tour bus spends with an animal, according to one study, is two minutes, and the average park visit lasts barely more than a night. Notes taken by Audubon photographer Page Chichester as for two hours he watched tourists watching a lioness in Kenya's Amboseli Park show how different is today's safari from those of the near and distant past:

4 P.M. — the lioness is resting in flatlands on the west side of Ol Turkai Swamp, mouth open, letting the cool breeze blow through.

4:05 — she is nearly run over by a white Suzuki, which remains.

4:25 — large, open truck with some 15 young humans arrives to gawk; two minibuses are attracted by the gathering and join in.

A lioness interrupts her gaping-mouthed rest outside Ol Turkai Arok Swamp to study a distant movement. Among elephants, lions are a danger only to calves and to sick, weak, or very unlucky adults. Lions number among the "big five" of safari animals, along with rhinos, buffalo, leopards, and elephants.

4:47—large truck leaves.

4:55—two minibuses leave, passing on the sighting, via radio, to a bus on the way.

5:10—bus arrives, revs engine twice, hoping for some alert or at least awake look from lioness; doesn't get it; nearly gets stuck; *all units, all units: lioness at Ol Turkai West*; all units converge.

5:15—three more buses arrive and are gone by 5:17.

5:25—six more buses arrive, staying one and a half minutes; two more hover on the horizon.

5:27—four more arrive, three or four leave, two more get the message.

5:29—another bus leaves; six remain; another arrives and stays quite awhile—two minutes already.

5:31—one leaves, then another.

5:32—another goes . . . and another; now there are three, all in a group.

5:33—one is coming, and two are on the horizon.

5:34—one bus starts to go, reverses—one last picture with the motor running; lioness continues sleeping.

5:35—a bus arrives.

5:36—two more cars . . . a bus . . . a Jeep . . . arrive; very loud French tourists, *Mon Dieu!* whistling, cat calls, and general babbling, motors running.

5:37—one bus starts and leaves . . . then another; a last call, *Woo-oo*; the Jeep leaves; three vehicles remain.

5:40—the bus with 10 French tourists leaves; another bus comes.

5:41—one leaves, another starts and leaves . . . no, stops again to talk to other driver; they leave; now we are two.

5:43—one goes, two are coming.

5:44—the first of the pair arrives, motor running; he moves into a better position and cuts the motor; the other bus is behind, photographing some wading birds.

5:45—the second bus arrives and cuts its motor.

5:46—the second bus starts again to reposition, cuts motor again.

5:48—another bus arrives, stops, lets motor run; lioness rolls over, back legs in the air, drawing laughs and comments; motor is still running; back legs go down.

5:49—lioness looks up, neither startled by nor interested in its audience; the motor is still running; now four other cars join the crowd; Running Motor backs up to go.

5:50—a motor starts . . . and another; one bus backs up and goes; the second follows suit; now a third; for the first time since 4:05 P.M. the lioness is alone; nothing on the horizon.

6:12—a bus arrives, tries to find the lioness and can't; lioness looks up, giving herself away.

6:13—last bus leaves without cutting motor.

Tourism, despite what appear to be its shortcomings, offers the promise of a future for African wildlife. Tourists bring valuable income to Africa, making the protection of wildlife important to African nations. Without tourism many species might simply be allowed to fade into extinction. This is almost certainly true of

Sitting upon a roadside rock, this yellow baboon was treated to apple sections and witty remarks thrown from tour vans.

the elephant, whose need for vast amounts of food can put it into conflict with Africa's increasingly large numbers of farmers and whose ivory is valued in world trade. Only its economic importance as a tourist attraction makes the elephant's protection essential in modern Africa.

Camera-toting tourists speeding down African game trails are not the only newcomers to the bush. The last few decades have seen the rise of a new scientific cadre, field biologists who are devoting their lives to studying African wildlife in the bush. Modern field biology dates largely from the late 1950s or early 1960s,

Modern African tourists do not think firearms are an essential accoutrement for a good time. Early risers are rewarded with the sight of a large bull elephant in soft morning light, a cloud-free Mt. Kilimanjaro in the distance. Such unforgettable images are the finest momentos of African safaris.

An elephant eats lush grass, pulling it from the swampy ground, roots and all. Only the palatable parts will be consumed.

beginning with such classic studies as biologist George Schaller's work with mountain gorillas and lions and Jane Goodall's research on chimpanzees. Until biologists such as these reached the field, much of what was known about African wildlife had been gleaned from the superficial observations of hunters and from dissection of dead animals. Modern field biology focuses on living animals and is characterized by years of observation of animals in the wild. Scientists are unlocking some of the deepest secrets of animal life, replacing with empirical data many of the myths and misunderstandings generated by the "expert" white hunters, whose biological knowledge was limited mainly to the basic information needed to get an animal under a gun sight. One animal that has received a great deal of scientific attention during the past quarter century is the elephant.

THE HIDDEN
WORLD OF THE
AFRICAN
ELEPHANT

"What happens is that people don't know, and so they can't help me," he was saying calmly. "But when they open their morning newspapers and see that thirty thousand elephants are being killed every year to make paper knives and billiard balls, and that there's a man who's doing his damnedest to stop this mass murder, they'll raise hell. When they hear that out of a hundred baby elephants captured for the zoos eighty die in the first days, you'll see what public opinion will say. There's such a thing as popular feeling, you know. That's the kind of thing that makes a government fall, I tell you. All that's needed is for the people to know."

Romain Gary, *The Roots of Heaven*

Elephants are a great tourist attraction and earn large amounts of foreign currency. Their ivory, hides and meat also fetch a high price. But one would, I think, have to be very limited in outlook to insist that their preservation can only be justified on commercial grounds. Economics are only one aspect of human ecology and though this approach is no less rational than the others, if adopted alone it is an impoverished philosophy which takes no account of the pleasure and interest which men can derive from elephants. It is like judging the artistic merit of the Mona Lisa by its current market value.

Iain and Oria Douglas-Hamilton, *Among the Elephants*

In the last two years I have realized that more than anything else, more than scientific discoveries or acceptance, what I care about and what I will fight for is the conservation, for as long as possible, not of just a certain number of elephants, but of the whole way of life of elephants. My priority, my love, my life are the Amboseli elephants, but I also want to ensure that there are elephants in other places that are able to exist in all the complexity and joy that elephants are capable of. It may be a lot to ask as we are about to enter the twenty-first century, but I think it is a goal worth striving for.

Cynthia Moss, *Elephant Memories: Thirteen Years in the
Life of an Elephant Family*

FOR THOSE BORN WITH A CRAVING TO SEE WILDLY, inconceivably exotic animals—who lament that they came along about a hundred million years too late to witness tyrannosaurs and diplodocuses and herds of triceratops—for these bereft people nature has created, by way of compensation, the elephant.

Growing up with elephants in our lives—seeing them in zoos and on safari and in film—makes it possible to forget how truly strange and exotic the elephant is, what a rare beast we have in it, and how fortunate connoisseurs of exotic animals are to have the elephant to savor.

It would be hard to dream up a more unlikely creature. An animal that stands up to 13 feet tall and weighs up to 12,000 pounds but that, as its skeleton shows, walks on the very tips of its toes. That has a nose about 8 feet long, a prehensile nose no less, one with which it can pick up things. An animal that in fact drinks with its nose, capable of drawing nearly a gallon of water into its nostrils and then draining the water into its mouth. That nose is a highly original evolutionary creation. No other creature has anything like it. If it seems commonplace, it is probably only because we call the elephant's nose a trunk, a special name for a special appendage. But when you think of it as an immense *nose,* its singularity becomes evident.

Stranger still is elephant dentition. Elephants have immense molars that grow one after another in sequence, the last one appearing when the animal is about 30 years old. Particularly exotic are the two upper incisors, which grow to be many feet long. We call them tusks, but they are in fact incisors, and no other animal has incisors like them. Nothing the dinosaurs offered is quite as impressive as incisors that potentially could grow up to 20 feet long.

The African elephant has the biggest ears in the animal king-

An unlikely beast, the elephant, with an 8-foot nose, the biggest ears in the animal kingdom, and incisors capable of growing up to 20 feet long. Males reach in excess of 12 feet at the shoulder and 12,000 pounds, making the elephant the largest living land animal.

(OPPOSITE)

This bull elephant on display in the Smithsonian's natural history museum stood 13 feet 2 inches tall and weighed about 12,000 pounds. The largest elephant on record, and quite possibly a contender for the title of "largest creature to walk the face of the Earth in the past 5,000 years," he was shot in Angola in 1955.

An Amboseli National Park elephant gives the air a cautionary sniff to ensure that all's well. In addition to its other fine qualities, the trunk is an excellent device for smelling.

dom. Probably the biggest ears ever. But then size is its stock in trade. It is the largest living land mammal. Its heart alone weighs about 60 pounds.

It is an excellent swimmer for a mammal, appears to be almost hairless, lives nearly 70 years, and sometimes buries its dead—all attributes that, oddly enough, make elephants sound something like humans.

Elephants resemble humans in other ways—in their close family ties, in their long maturational process, in their handing down of knowledge from generation to generation. These similarities are, in many ways, artifacts imposed by evolution upon species that lead long and highly social lives, including wolves and almost all monkeys and apes. But these similarities also inspire human

interest in these creatures and in their behavior. Even in elephants we see biological reflections of ourselves, echoes that permit us to take some measure of our relation to and separation from other creatures, to learn which characteristics truly make us us, and which are merely traits that all social mammals have in common, because without them they would not survive.

Africa is home to two types of elephants, the savannah or bush elephant, which scientists have labelled *Loxodonta africana africana*, and the forest elephant, *Loxodonta africana cyclotis*. The forest elephant tends to be smaller than the bush variety, standing 8 feet tall or less at the shoulder, compared to the bush elephant's maximum of about 13 feet. The forest elephant has relatively smaller ears, a rounded rather than a swayed back, and long, thin, straight tusks. The tusks have a pinkish hue and are said to be harder than bush elephant tusks. The hardness makes them more difficult to carve, because they shatter more easily.

There are almost certainly behaviorial differences between the two varieties. It is suspected, for example, that male forest elephants leave their maternal herd at a younger age than do bush elephants. Little is known about forest elephants, however, be-

A molar from an elephant that died during the 1970–71 drought at Kenya's Tsavo National Park. An elephant cuts six molars per jaw during its life, the last coming in when the animal is about 30 years old. Through constant grinding, the last set will wear down until useless, and the 60-odd-year-old elephant, unable to chew, will die of malnutrition. An elephant's age can be determined from the condition of its molars.

A yearling rubs his face in the dirt, performing three vital functions: covering his skin with sun-protecting dirt, rubbing off ticks and other parasites, and providing protection from further infestation.

cause they are very hard to study. They tend to live in forest so dense that, large as they are, they are impossible to see from as little as 30 feet away. They also tend to slip away quietly into the forest at the first sign of human intruders. Consequently most of what is known about elephant behavior has been gleaned from studies of the more readily observed bush elephant, the variety that is by far the most commonly seen and filmed.

The study of elephant behavior is in its infancy, but a great deal has already been learned. Modern elephant behavioral research began in 1965 with a study by British biologist Iain Douglas-Hamilton on the elephants of Lake Manyara National Park in northern Tanzania. No one had ever done a long, detailed behavioral study on elephants until Douglas-Hamilton did his. Previous work, such as that begun in the early 1960s by biologist Richard Laws, dealt primarily with elephant anatomy and physiology. Laws worked with Ian Parker, a former professional hunter for the Kenya Game Department who killed hundreds upon hundreds of elephants in culling operations. After Parker quit the Game Department, he started a private business, Wild Life Services, which paid about $12 per animal for the right to slaughter elephants in

Assistant warden and research biologist Samuel M. Kasiki examines one of several thousand jaws from elephants that died in the 1970–71 drought in Tsavo National Park. The collection is probably the largest in the world. At about the time that the drought killed some 9,000 Tsavo elephants, ivory prices rose, leading to intensified poaching that nearly put the finishing touches on once-uncountable numbers.

Elephant researcher Iain Douglas-Hamilton talks with British journalists at Tsavo East National Park headquarters. He is explaining that the maps correlate distributions of humans, tsetse flies, and elephants. People usually avoid tsetse fly areas, because the insects carry diseases deadly to humans. Consequently, elephant numbers tend to be higher in places infested with the flies. Douglas-Hamilton, who started studying elephants in 1965, was the first to document the animals' complex social and family structures.

areas where they were thought to be overpopulated or where farmlands were encroaching on the bush and drawing the attention of hungry elephants. Parker killed about 2,000 elephants and made a tidy profit selling ivory, meat, hides, and even feet that had been turned into umbrella stands and waste baskets.

He also provided Laws with the opportunity to dissect hundreds of elephants, and in this way Laws was able to determine how elephants mature physiologically and deduce information about their breeding patterns. By studying dentition on captive animals of a known age, and correlating this data with the dentition of some 400 jaws from wild elephants, he was able to develop techniques by which the age of a wild elephant could be determined, based on the condition of its molars. Though this was a useful technique when working with dead animals, it was less than illuminating in the study of live elephants. So Laws's next task was correlating tooth growth with body growth. Using measurements from elephants shot for research, and matching the measurements with dentition, Laws was able to determine the height of an elephant at a given age. This allowed him to produce a growth curve showing the average height at a given age. Though some variation in size existed among elephants of the same age, size correlated closely enough with age to make it a reliable indicator of age up to 15 years old, perhaps older in males. Further refinements permitted researchers to estimate roughly an elephant's age by measuring the diameter of the track left by the hind foot.

All this information was useful, but it cost the lives of many elephants. It also failed to provide much information on elephant social behavior and ecology, which was Douglas-Hamilton's goal. He consequently studied living animals, using the knowledge accrued by Laws and focusing on herds of adult females and their offspring. He thus developed the first clear picture of elephant social behavior. He also popularized research techniques that have proved indispensible to other elephant biologists. Primary among these was his discovery that individual elephants could be recognized by their ears. The general shape of the ear, its size, and, more importantly, various scars, tears, and holes serve to distinguish individual elephants. Most significant, however, are the veins that lace the ears with characteristic patterns that never change. Like fingerprints in humans, the indelible vein patterns are a reliable means for identifying individual elephants.

To make use of the ears, Douglas-Hamilton photographed the elephants he studied from all angles. This was no easy task, since he had to maneuver among animals clustering in herds. The elephants could not be counted on to provide him with frontal, right-side, and left-side shots. Hamilton therefore took an approach that might have been lauded by William Cotton Oswell. He would approach his photographic subjects until he crossed their pachydermal line of personal space. Then the elephants would turn and threaten him, their ears outstretched in a precharge display. Hamilton would immediately snap a picture and race to climb straight up the nearest tree, since a charge was likely to follow. Oria Douglas-Hamilton, Iain's wife, said he be-

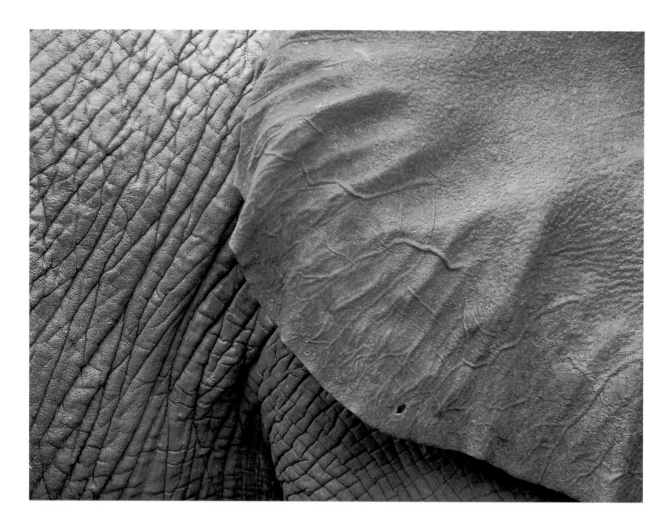

Ear shape and vein-patterns are two important characteristics that help field researchers identify individuals in their study area. The importance of ears in identification was discovered by Iain Douglas-Hamilton in the 1960s.

came very good at climbing trees. Eventually he built up a photographic file that allowed him and other biologists to identify nearly 500 elephants at Manyara. His technique also has been adopted by other researchers.

One student who worked with Douglas-Hamilton was Cynthia Moss, a former reporter and researcher for *Newsweek* magazine who in 1968 moved to Africa and started a new career as a biologist. She worked with Douglas-Hamilton and learned from him the ear-identification technique before going on to study the elephants of Amboseli National Park in Kenya. Her study, begun in 1972, continues to this day, and she is providing vital new details on the lives of wild African elephants.

Moss's work has attracted the interest and participation of many other biologists, who, by studying various aspects of elephant behavior, are elucidating the entire gamut of elephant life. Perhaps foremost among them are Joyce Poole and Katherine Payne. Poole is the daughter of a former director of the African Wildlife Foundation and started working with Moss in 1975, when she was a 19-year-old student on vacation from college. Poole has continued working with Amboseli elephants, studying

THE HIDDEN WORLD OF THE AFRICAN ELEPHANT

the sexual patterns of male African elephants, particularly in their periodic states of heightened sexual behavior and aggression.

Katherine Payne spent a dozen years studying sound communication in whales, particularly humpbacks, before turning to elephants in 1984. While observing a group of elephants in a zoo in Portland, Oregon, she found that the animals seemed rarely to vocalize. But because she sometimes felt a throbbing sensation when near the apparently silent elephants, as one might feel from distant thunder, she guessed that elephants, like some whales, might produce infrasounds, which are sounds below the level of human hearing. Using special recording equipment loaned her by Cornell University, she determined that the elephants were indeed using infrasound. In order to hear the sounds they produced, she speeded up her recordings tenfold.

Payne went to Amboseli National Park in 1985. Working with Joyce Poole, she made recordings which indicated that African elephants did indeed communicate among themselves with infrasound. Many of the calls were up to 6 seconds long, and some were uttered in a series that might last for 10 minutes. This was the first evidence that a land mammal used infrasound communication. The discovery helped explain how elephants miles apart

Joyce Poole (left) and Cynthia Moss watch elephants feeding in the swamp behind their research camp in Ol Turkai Arok in Amboseli National Park. Their combined work represents some 35 years of elephant study.

Cynthia Moss's headquarters, the African Elephant Research Project camp in Ol Turkai Swamp, offers a stunning view of Mt. Kilimanjaro, some 31 miles across the Kenyan border in Tanzania. The bleached skull beneath the tree is from an elephant.

are able to coordinate their movements, even though they produce no signals apparent to humans: Some infrasounds can carry for miles.

Old-time white hunters often referred to the stomach rumbles made by elephants as they digested their food. Careful field observations have shown that these rumbles are a type of communication and originate in the larynx. They have nothing to do with digestion. Poole's studies at Amboseli have identified 17 different rumbles that have infrasound components. Still other rumbles consist entirely of infrasounds below the level of human hearing.

Most studies have focused on the bush elephant. Research on

(OPPOSITE)
An adult wades through high grass in Amboseli National Park, where biologist Cynthia Moss conducts her research. The park, encompassing only about 150 square miles, has some 700 elephants and has seen almost no poaching the past 10 years. Lack of poaching makes the animals less frightened of people and therefore easier to approach, study, and observe.

Dionysis, a large Amboseli bull called M-22 for research purposes, feeds in early-morning light beneath the gaze of snowcapped Mt. Kilimanjaro.

the forest elephant is only now getting under way. Richard and Karen Barnes, a husband and wife team funded by the New York Zoological Society's research division, Wildlife Conservation International, have undertaken the daunting task of censuing the elephant population in the forests of Gabon. When they have perfected their techniques, they want to move on to forests in other nations and, with the help of other biologists, complete a reliable estimate of the forest elephant population. They are also beginning to scratch the surface of forest elephant behavior.

These biologists and others who have spent long months or years in the field have, in the past 25 years, brought us more real knowledge about elephants than was known in all of previous history. What they are learning and teaching reveals an animal unexpectedly complex in its behavior and in its need for a stable social life, a stability increasingly tenuous as humans crowd more and more deeply into the heart of Africa.

Elephants appear to enjoy giving one leg a break from time to time and will often stand with one leg crossed over the other while feeding or resting.

█ BEHOLD NOW BEHEMOTH: THE ELEPHANT OF AFRICA

Elephants are born after 22 months of gestation into a stable family group made up of related adult female elephants and their immature offspring. The size of a family unit presumably depends at least in part on what the habitat will bear, but in studies by Moss and Douglas-Hamilton the average family unit was about 10 animals. These are stable groups that form the basic unit of elephant society, at least for females.

Each of these family groups is led by an old female that researchers call the matriarch. Other adult females in the herd are her sisters, cousins, daughters or granddaughters or perhaps her nieces and grandnieces. The matriarchs in unpoached populations are usually quite old, in their forties, fifties, sixties. They are great reservoirs of valuable, perhaps even irreplaceable, experience and knowledge. After decades of life, each matriarch knows the best places to seek food and water, even during droughts, and which areas to avoid because of human encroachment. Each leads her family, determining when and where it will travel. When danger threatens, the rest of the family rallies behind her, awaiting her reaction before deciding what to do.

The importance of the family to the well-being of the individual elephant cannot be overestimated. Elephants are extremely social, so much so that the actions of group members are nearly always synchronized. They usually feed, wash, drink, and rest together. Mothers and offspring are rarely separated by more than a few yards and are often touching. The adults often touch one another, too, caressing with trunks or leaning together. Older female calves frequently care for younger calves, sealing a relationship among individuals of different generations. When individuals do become physically separated, they remain in contact through vocal communication.

Virtually all family groups have important social ties to certain other families with which they frequently associate. Individuals from these closely bonded families greet one another, the young play with each other, and all may feed and travel together and frequently touch one another. Because the oldest elephants may be in their sixties, and elephant research is only in its twenties, biologists are not certain about the nature of the bonds that exist among different families. Perhaps the matriarchs of the different herds are elderly cousins or sisters. Presumably, some close relationship exists and, for that reason, Moss refers to these families as bond groups. If elephants and elephant research survive, spec-

An elephant group gathers by a dead acacia tree, used as a rubbing post. *(OPPOSITE)*

A calf gets down and dirty at a Tsavo East watering hole. Having waited his turn, he plumped himself down and started playing with his trunk and the water. Such games also serve a useful purpose: protecting the calf's dehydration-prone skin from the relentless African sun.

ulation on these relationships will perhaps be replaced by empirical information in the next century.

The social dynamics of the family groups are not clear either,
though it is known that some groups result from the break-up of
large families. Moss, in her excellent and readable book *Elephant
Memories,* tells of one herd of 29 individuals, roughly three times
the average size for an Amboseli herd. Over a two-year period,
this family broke into two herds, each led by a matriarch of its
own. Why the fragmentation occurred is not clear. Perhaps the
big herd was socially unwieldy, or the environment could not
sustain such a large number of elephants feeding together. In any
event, the elephants maintained their special bonds, continuing
to interact after the split and occasionally even regrouping. Douglas-Hamilton observed similar splits in large herds at Manyara. In
one case a relatively young matriarch split off with four other
elephants from a herd of 22, apparently to avoid competition with
two old females in the big herd.

In any event, the newborn calf's most stable social environment is the family group. At 260 pounds and something under 3
feet tall, the newborn, though tuskless, is otherwise nearly a per-

Bond-group members feed
among the bush in Tsavo East
National Park near Voi. A bond-
group is a number of elephant
families that remain together over
long periods, moving in a
coordinated manner and
displaying familiarity among one
another. Researcher Cynthia Moss
suspects the bond-groups are
made up of extended families, but
her 15-year research project has
not been under way long enough
to prove her theory.

87

fect miniature of an adult. The calf has a long period of growth ahead of it before it reaches adult size—nearly two decades for females, longer for males. If the calf is a female, it weighs about 4 percent of its adult weight. A male calf weighs only 2 percent of its adult weight. For this reason, males, needing more food and energy to grow, suckle more often than females. The need for larger amounts of food makes them highly vulnerable to stress. During drought years, when hunger travels constantly with the family groups, significantly more male than female calves perish.

The calf also needs energy for internal development. Its brain is about a third of its adult weight of 10 pounds, in contrast to most mammals in which the weight of the brain at birth is about 90 percent of its adult weight. This suggests that the calf requires a long period of dependency during which its nervous system matures and develops the capacities and coordination needed for adult life. The calf cannot survive without its family to rear it.

The newborn calf can walk about 45 minutes after its birth and, though scarcely able to see, will follow on the heels of its mother, locating her by scent and sound. At birth the calf may have patches of red or black hair on its forehead, head, and back. The red hair is reminiscent of the old mammoths and may show some ancient link to that breed.

A mother and her offspring feed side-by-side in Amboseli's Ol Turkai Arok Swamp. A female may remain with her family until she dies, or she may break away to become matriarch of her own family group. Even if she does form a separate group, she and her followers will probably continue to associate with her old family, forming what researchers call a bond-group.

Elephants take a noontime nap in the shade of acacia and palm trees near their swampy feeding grounds. While resting, elephants will sometimes drape their trunks over their tusks, possibly to protect them from ground-roving insects.

A mother moves her right foreleg forward, making it easier for her week-old male calf to suckle. The calf will breast-feed until a sibling is born in about four years.

A week-old calf basks in the security of his mother's shadow. This habit protects the vulnerable newborns from dehydration and predators. Calves spend most of their time below or beside their mothers. In fact, one field test for a calf's age is whether it can stand under its mother.

A youngster rests under palm and acacia trees, avoiding intense midday sun. Dehydration is a serious threat to young elephants. The group will rest for an hour or so before continuing its eating routine. An adult elephant sleeps only about four hours a day.

The calf during the first months of life will spend fully 99 percent of its time in contact with its mother. It will rarely stray more than a foot away from her and will often touch her with trunk or body. It will also stay near other female relatives. Should it wander off for any reason, the mother or an older female calf will usually follow it. Any cry of alarm from the baby will instantly bring all family group to the rescue.

The calf begins learning to use its trunk in the first week of life. Ceaselessly exploring, it touches objects new to it and tries to pick up sticks and grass. The African elephant has two finger-like projections on the tip of the trunk with which it can pick up even tiny twigs, but using the trunk skillfully to grasp small objects takes practice. Baby elephants tend to be as inept as baby humans at manipulating their environment.

At about three months, the calf will begin spending increasing amounts of time handling (trunkling?) vegetation and at about that age will start eating grass. However, it will be inordinately slow at feeding. During the time it takes the calf to pick up and eat a single blade of grass, the adults around it will munch down nine full trunk loads. Over the next few months, the calf will learn to eat more vegetable food, until at nine months it is spending nearly half its life foraging. Even then the calf will continue to suckle the two breasts that, swollen with milk, bulge between its mother's front legs. The calf will also take food from the mouths of older elephants or eat food that they drop. Apparently this process teaches it which plants to eat.

A very young calf will kneel to drink water with its mouth, just as it will occasionally kneel to graze. But at four months it begins to experiment with sucking water up into its trunk and then releasing the water into its mouth. Within another month or so it will be fairly skilled at this technique.

The calf will play with other calves in the herd. This presumably is an important process by which the calves establish social bonds and learn skills that they will use later in life. For example, calves often spar with one another, butting their heads together. This may help males develop skills they will use later in fighting for position in the male heirarchy.

In its early months, the baby calf is tolerated and indulged by the rest of the family, but as it matures it is indulged less and less. It begins to learn the social hierarchy of the herd, finding out how it relates to other members and to whom it should defer. It will also learn over the years the daily and seasonal routes that the herd travels in its endless quest for food, water, and resting places.

At about two years of age, the calf's tusks begin to appear. The

Elephants draw water into their trunks before tipping back their heads, raising their trunks, and letting the water flow down their throats. An elephant can draw nearly a gallon of water at a time. Calves must learn this craft, going down on their knees to drink until they have mastered the trick.

This calf was nearly crippled at birth, with his front legs bent in a kneeling position. He had to sit to reach his mother's teats. By stretching he was able to limp; within a week he could walk, albeit stiffly.

tusks are modified incisors. They are tipped with enamel, but the rest of the tusk is dentine. The tusks grow throughout the elephant's life and could reach 16 feet long in a female and 20 in a male. However, they virtually never reach these sizes because elephants use them for a wide variety of tasks that wear them down. They use them to chip bark from and knock down trees, to dig, and to fight one another. And because each elephant tends to favor either the right or left tusk, just as the right or left hand dominates in people, one tusk is usually more worn than the other.

Despite the wear and tear, elephants can grow some imposing sets of tusks. In 1874, when more big tuskers survived than do today, a tusk sold in London weighed 188 pounds. Another tusk from about the same period weighed 184 pounds, with a length

(OPPOSITE)
An adult male wraps his trunk around a bunch of grass before ripping it from the ground. The trunk tip is filled with nerve endings and is said to be sensitive enough to read braille.

Sub-adults play-fight, an exercise that reinforces group bonds and sets the pecking order. The activity also teaches skills that will be important in later life.

of 9 feet 5 inches and a girth of 22 and ½ inches. The longest on record, also from the late 1800s, weighed only 173 pounds but was 20 feet 9 inches long. The heaviest known tusks are in the British Museum of Natural History. They were taken from an old bull shot near Mount Kilimanjaro in 1897 and, when fresh, together weighed 460 pounds. Drying has reduced their weight to 440 pounds. The heavy killing of elephants for ivory in recent years has greatly reduced average tusk size. Tusks more than 30 pounds apiece are considered large today. The average is about 13 pounds.

As calves mature, the lives of males and females diverge. A female usually stays with her mother's herd all her life. At about 11 or 12 years, though still only about 65 percent of her adult

Bathed in warm, late-afternoon sun, an adult bull browses among bushes and shrubs in Tsavo East National Park. Elephants use their tusks for a variety of tasks, such as digging and knocking down trees, and usually use one tusk more than the other. The wear on this bull's ivory shows that he favors his left tusk.

After a half-hour rest on its side, a calf in Amboseli National Park works his way into an upright position. Unlike adults, who sleep standing, calves usually sleep on their sides.

height of 8 feet and weighing considerably less than her adult weight of 6,000 pounds, a female reaches sexual maturity. At that age, if in estrus, she might mate with a wandering bull elephant visiting the group in search of receptive females. Nearly two years later, she would give birth to her first calf. If food resources were good and the calf survived, the mother would be ready to mate again in two more years and would produce another calf when the first was four years old. She would probably continue to give birth every four or five years until she was 50. After that the birth rate would slow and any calves born to her might fail to survive. In her late 50s, the mother would enter old age. By then she might be the matriarch of her family, having succeeded her mother or another older relative. By the time she is 65, her last molar, which has been grinding away daily for 35 years, is about worn out. The mother elephant gradually becomes unable to chew her food, and slowly her energy ebbs and her life comes to an end.

The life of a male calf is quite different. He reaches sexual maturity at 17 years. Sometime before his twentieth year—and generally by his fourteenth—he leaves his family. For a while he stays nearby, following the family in the company of other young bulls. But then he begins to drift away, alternately returning to his family and joining all-male herds that probably live in areas removed from the females. There he learns the dominance hierarchy and discovers who he can overrule and to whom he must defer.

Dominance is based on size, and, because elephants grow throughout life, the older males tend to be dominant. They generally use their social position to keep young bulls from breeding. Even if they did not, the younger bulls still might find it difficult to find a mate, since receptive females do not want to mate with young bulls.

When the young bull reaches 30, he is approaching full male size—up to 12 feet tall at the shoulder, though perhaps still some distance from the mature weight of six tons. At around this age he experiences for the first time a sudden explosion in testosterone levels that puts him into a breeding condition called *musth*, an Urdu word meaning intoxicated. It is a wisely chosen term. Testosterone is a male sex hormone and, in bull elephants experiencing the high testosterone levels of musth, it heightens both the sex drive and hostility toward other males. A bull in musth becomes much more willing to fight for access to a receptive female.

A bull in musth bears several telltale signs. His temporal

glands, located on the side of the head, swell and secrete a thick fluid that streams down his face. He begins to dribble urine constantly as he moves from place to place. His gait lengthens and becomes more purposeful, and he produces a special low frequency vocalization, the musth rumble, which is a sort of love song to cows and a warning to bulls. All the various scents, fluids, noises, and poses made by the musth bull presumably serve to advertise his condition, attracting females and keeping other bulls out of the way.

The musth bull's willingness to fight and fight hard, even to the death, alters his position in the dominance hierarchy. A musth bull can dominate all others that are not in musth, including larger bulls. In confrontations between musth and nonmusth bulls, the nonmusth bull tends to defer even if he is the larger of the two.

A large male strolls toward heavy cover, probably seeking shade from the hot midday sun. Adult bulls travel alone or in small, all-male groups, joining the matriarchal families only to breed.

Swollen temporal glands oozing a thick substance indicate that this bull is in musth, a period of heightened sexual urges and aggression. The musth bull's win-or-die attitude in competing for females permits it to dominate non-musth males, even bulls to which it normally is submissive. This bull is reaching his peak mating period in March, a prime season because many females are in estrus.

Fights between musth bulls can last for hours, with the animals threatening one another and intermittently locking tusks and trying to twist one another to the ground, where the fallen bull will be open to a stabbing attack. Some fights last for hours, leaving the bulls overheated and exhausted. Sometimes one of them is killed. Young musth bulls usually avoid old musth bulls, and sometimes harassment by the old bulls can suppress musth in younger males. The old bulls generally avoid fighting each other, however. They do this by entering musth at different times or by operating in different areas.

A bull 25 to 35 years old will enter sporadic periods of musth lasting only a a few days to a few weeks. In older bulls, musth occurs at a predictable time each year and lasts for two to five months.

A musth bull will approach cow groups in search of females in breeding condition, or *estrus.* When he finds a receptive female, he will breed with her and probably stay with her for two or three days. Most of the breeding is done by males 35 or older, since females seem to prefer the older males. Presumably this is

The losing bull in a confrontation retreats *post haste* after a standoff in Amboseli National Park. Serious fights between bulls are rare, but can last for hours and produce deadly results.

A male in musth greets a female, then tests her by putting his trunk tip to her vulva and tasting it to see if she is in estrus. If she is receptive, he may mount her, remaining and copulating with her for several days.

advantageous to the female for several reasons. By breeding with an older bull, she is more certain that her calf will inherit the genes of an old, successful adult, bestowing upon it the healthy physique and successful behaviors that make for a long life. On a more immediate level, the older musth bull gives her some relief from the numerous young musth males that gather around fe-males in estrous. Young males often pursue estrous females end-lessly, wearing them down. Older bulls will frighten away the younger ones, and the female, as long as she stays near the old bull, will be able to rest.

The older, most dominant bulls tend to breed with females that are at the height of estrus. Females exhibit estrous behavior for four to six days. At the onset of estrus, the females tend to run

A bull and female feed on lush rainy-season grasses in Tsavo East National Park near Voi. Bulls rely on a keen sense of smell and acute hearing to locate females in estrus. If he is a full-grown, dominant male past 40 he may stay with the female a few days, providing her protection from young, over-eager males.

One bull chases another from a watering hole after peacefully drinking beside him. Dominance defines all aspects of elephant interaction.

from the younger bulls and cause a commotion that presumably attracts the older musth bulls. During the middle two to three days of estrus the cow is most fertile and usually will breed and consort with an older musth bull. During this time the large musth bull guards the cow from younger bulls. As the cow moves out of estrus the old bull loses interest, and the cow may be once again subject to the overtures of the young bulls, which she again tries to avoid.

The old bulls are critical to the success of elephant reproduction, a fact that eluded many early observers who were, of course, woefully short of reliable knowledge about elephant behavior. Much of what the early hunters thought they knew was based on speculation and on extrapolation from the behavior of better known animals, such as deer. Thus when writing of the ivory trade and its effect on elephant populations in some parts of Africa, Theodore Roosevelt was able to observe with complete but groundless confidence in *African Game Trails* that "the elephant have not greatly diminished in aggregate numbers, although the number of bulls carrying big ivory has been very much reduced; indeed the reproductive capacity of the herds has probably been very little impaired, the energies of the hunters having been almost exclusively directed to the killing of the bulls with tusks weighing over 30 pounds apiece; and the really big tuskers, which are most eagerly sought after, are almost always past their prime, and no longer associate with the herd." We know now that the old bulls wandering in male herds or alone are generally *in* their prime, not past it, and that they do associate with the female groups when in musth. Lack of reliable knowledge about wildlife often leads to misguided management plans for various species. Elephants, in some areas subject to government-planned culls designed to reduce herd numbers, are probably among the foremost species victimized by human ignorance and overconfidence.

Musth is not an easy time for a bull elephant. He spends most of his time searching for cows and fighting other bulls. After two or three months of musth, the bull loses considerable weight. When musth ends it is a much thinner bull that returns to his bull area.

▌ ELEPHANT ECOLOGY: CULLS AND CONTROVERSY

Elephants eat vast quantities of food every day. They can pack away 770 pounds of vegetable food daily and top it off with 40 gallons of water. They eat a wide variety of grasses and also browse on bushes and trees. The percentage of grass and browse in their diet is seasonal. During wet seasons they may eat primarily grasses, but when dry seasons or prolonged droughts occur, grasses decline and elephants are compelled to rely more on bushes and trees for food. Because elephants frequently browse by uprooting bushes and trees, some wildlife managers have feared that elephants will ruin their habitat during droughts. Such fears were fueled by research in the early 1970s that indicated that a single elephant might push down 1,000 trees each year. At this rate, some studies have suggested, certain types of woodlands begin to shrink. Given these figures and the ruined look—to human eyes, anyway—of areas heavily used by elephants during droughts and dry seasons, some wildlife managers have con-

cluded that some elephant herds need to be culled to protect trees.

Culling usually involves the shooting of entire family groups, with the possible exception of calves young enough to be sold to zoos. Professional hunters armed with automatic weapons conduct the culls. They try to creep close to a feeding herd and make a few small noises to alarm the animals. The elephants then gather near the matriarch. Once the animals congregate, they can be easily slaughtered. A skilled hunter can wipe out a family of 10 or 12 elephants in roughly 30 seconds. The ivory can then be collected for sale and the meat distributed to native peoples or sold. Hides are used for leather, and even the feet can be sold for stools or umbrella stands.

Culling is not restricted to elephants. In Kruger National Park in South Africa, for example, some 11,306 animals were killed in a five-year cull operation that targeted elephants, rhinos, hippos, and buffalo. However, because of the extensive damage that elephants seem to do to woodlands, they have long been a major target. For example, in the 1970s hundreds of elephants were killed in Zimbabwe's Hwange National Park, where a few thousand are still targeted for slaughter whenever park woodlands seem jeopardized.

Culling is the subject of great scientific debate, dividing elephant biologists into pro- and anti-cull camps. Of the many arguments that surround the culls, perhaps the most haunting is the possibility that human attempts to trim herds are based on the same arrogance and ignorance that kept Roosevelt from recognizing the biological importance of old bull elephants. Many biologists are disturbed by the idea that the species that brought us global warming and ozone depletion is now going to take upon itself responsibility for balancing African ecosystems.

Those who favor culls are convinced that woodland destruction by elephants will have harmful effects not only on the habitat, but also on all the wildlife species dependent upon woodlands. In other words, browsing elephants may threaten an entire ecosystem. Cull opponents respond that the declines in woodlands brought about by elephants are part of a natural cycle of ebb and flow, with elephants now increasing as woodlands decline, and elephants then declining as woodlands regrow. As Brian Walker, of the Center for Resource Ecology in Johannesburg, South Africa, wrote in *Problems in Management of Locally Abundant Wild Mammals*, "Very often, many of our management actions which are aimed at conserving ecosystems and species are the opposite of what we should do. We cull animals when they increase, and

(OPPOSITE)
A big bull, feeding after a storm in Tsavo East National Park, thrashes a bunch of grass against his trunk to shake off dirt before stuffing the vegetation into his mouth.

A young elephant feeds on branches of a downed acacia tree. The animal's thick skin seems impervious to the tree's long, sharp thorns. Some wildlife managers, convinced that elephants are wiping out trees at Amboseli, believe shooting the animals to reduce their number is the only way to protect woodlands. Others debunk the whole idea, saying a rising water table and increased salinity are responsible for tree declines.

The gnarled trunk of a standing acacia tree shows scars from elephant tusks.

Native African people may be a blessing or a curse to park wildlife. They often help game rangers locate poachers and report poaching activities. But as Africans turn from raising livestock to growing crops, conflicts with wildlife are increasing along park borders. Kenya Wildlife Service director Richard Leakey proposes extensive fencing along some borders to keep wildlife out of croplands.

A cattle egret keeps a sharp lookout for insects kicked up by his four-legged perch, an elephant. Elephants are tied to the survival of many other species. By knocking down trees, elephants can open up woodlands, making them more suitable for grazing antelope. Their ability to locate underground water and to dig pools helps provide many species with drink during droughts.

we save them or introduce more when they decrease, to keep things constant. We spread water supplies evenly all over the reserves to remove spatial variation, and we use patch burning for the same reason. Most of our actions are in fact aimed at preventing the variability in time and space which in all probability is essential for the maintenance of ecosystem resilience.''

Culling operations themselves do little to inspire confidence in skeptics. In the mid-1960s, for example, the wildebeest, a type of hoofed animal, was increasing during a dry period in South Africa's Kruger National Park. Since the habitat seemed to be declining, a wildebeest cull was started in 1965. In 1971 a wet period began, and two years later culling was stopped because wildebeest numbers seemed to be dropping too fast. Even after the culling ended, the animals continued to decline. Finally, in

Two cattle egrets hitchhike atop a large, feeding bull in Enkongo Narok Swamp. The swamp's name comes from the Maa (Maasai) word meaning "black eye."

A sub-adult in Amboseli National Park feeds on grass, which during certain times of year makes up the bulk of its diet. Elephants ingest about 770 pounds of vegetation daily, along with 30 to 50 gallons of water.

1979, the park started culling lions to protect the failing wildebeest. Wildlife managers finally concluded that wildebeests tend to do well during dry seasons, when grass is short and of high quality. Their numbers then increase. When wet seasons arrive, however, wildebeests tend to decline, in part because lions increase fourfold. Wildebeests apparently need dry season population explosions to survive the debilitating wet seasons.

Wiping out entire family groups may hold special dangers for elephants, since the groups may represent distinct genetic lines. Destroying a whole genetic line may have harmful effects that have not been recognized simply because no one has studied this possibility. Culling programs are driven purely by concerns about habitat and are conducted in complete ignorance of genetic effects. By wiping out genetic lines in a relatively small group of animals, genetic variation is quite likely to be lost, producing, ultimately, some of the harmful effects associated with inbreeding. Moreover, groups are fully together only 50 to 80 percent of the time. It is likely the culling of a group presumed to be an entire family in fact kills only a portion of the group, leaving fragmented families and causing increased calf mortality. Also, culling re-

An elephant gives its younger traveling companion a friendly nudge to speed up the tempo in an Amboseli woodland. The park's elephant population of about 700 is healthy and growing, causing concern that the elephants will destroy the park by killing the trees upon which they feed. Culling operations are being considered.

duces groups to less than the carrying capacity of the habitat. In reponse, reproduction increases, roping wildlife managers into an endless culling program as populations grow. Furthermore, culling reduces the overall age of an elephant population, posing another threat to elephant social survival.

In addition, some evidence suggests that the relationship between elephants and woodlands is not as simple as cull proponents believe. During a study of elephant dung in a park in Ghana, biologists discovered that many seeds from fruits eaten by elephants passed through the digestive tract unharmed. By eating seed-laden fruit, elephants helped disperse 11 different tree species throughout the park. Seeds from three tree species, tested in a laboratory, would not germinate without dung, and in others the dung contributed to a more rapid growth.

In another study it was found that about 75 percent of acacia seed pods that pass through an elephant's intestine germinate successfully, compared to only 12 percent for seeds that have not passed through an elephant. Apparently the digestive process softens the seeds' outer coverings and the dung provides fertilizer. This evidence suggests that while elephants sometimes destroy trees, they also may be crucial to woodland regeneration. The only certainty is that a great deal remains unknown. Justification for culling operations depends largely on how comfortable wildlife managers feel about predicating their actions on incomplete data and uncertain understanding. Apparently enough are comfortable with these conditions, since hundreds of elephants fall yearly to offical culling operations.

∎ ELEPHANT COMMUNICATION

Humans are unusual among mammals in that we lack a good sense of smell. Most mammal species have a well-developed sense of smell and are attuned to the myriad scents that waft across their world. The winds and breezes must be crowded with olfactory messages that humans cannot perceive. Indeed we are so removed from the world of scents that we do not even have a word for one who cannot smell, though we have "blind" for those who cannot see and "deaf" for those who cannot hear.

To fully understand elephant communication is difficult for human researchers. The limitations of our senses lock us out of the elephant's communication loop. Olfaction—the sense of smell—plays a very large part in elephant communication. Even our hearing is an obstacle to full understanding, since elephants hear sounds that we cannot. Nevertheless, biologists have made some fascinating and unexpected discoveries.

Conveying messages by means of scent is very useful, because it allows an animal to express itself even in its absence. This is perhaps shown best by the musth bulls. The secretions from their temporal glands are musky smelling and more copious and viscous than secretions from other elephants. Musth bulls rub their temporal glands against trees to leave a scent mark for other elephants. Musth bulls also dribble urine almost constantly, leaving a trail wherever they go. Presumably scent from the temporal glands and the urine communicates to other elephants that a musth bull is near, as well as how recently he passed by, who he is, and how deep in musth he is. Observations of other elephants

After giving a warning headshake, this young bull observes the photographer's reaction, creating a most intimidating posture with his wide-spread ears.

A young bull gives the photographer a warning head-shake. If the photographer doesn't flee, the elephant may charge, though it is more likely to beat an unheroic but safe retreat.

encountering urine trails or temporal gland scents indicate that this odor is used as a social signal. For example, when cow elephants come upon a musth bull's urine trail, they become excited. When young musth males encounter the scents of an older musth bull, they often respond by leaving the area or even slowing their own temporal secretions and urine dribbling. The use of odors may even work on a physiological level. Young bulls may go out of musth as a result of scenting an older musth bull, and, though this is speculation, it is possible that contact with the odors of a musth bull may cause a cow to go into estrus.

Musth bulls provide a good example of another form of elephant communication, body language. Musth males carry themselves in a distinct musth posture, walking with heads high and ears outspread and tensely held. Joyce Poole has said that she can recognize a musth bull by this posture from a distance of up to a mile.

Musth bulls also flap their ears in a peculiar style called an ear wave. They move only one ear at a time, with the upper and inner portion pulled forward powerfully while the lower and outer parts trail behind. This is seen most often when a bull musth rumbles or when two bulls are challenging each other. Ear movement may also waft scents from the temporal glands into the air.

Elephants use a wide variety of distinct types of ear flapping in their communications. When females are threatening one another, they fold under the lower portions of their ears with their heads extended. When individuals within a family or bond group greet one another after an absence, they flap their ears rapidly while holding their heads and ears high. Ears extended widely are generally associated with elephants attempting to bluff an opponent enemy. However, not all ear movements convey messages. Ears are also used in *thermoregulation*, the control of body temperature. Ears are relatively thin appendages laced with blood vessels. Flapping the ears helps cool the blood passing through them, which helps dissipate body heat.

The most exciting discoveries in the field of elephant communication concern vocal signals. Elephants use a wide number of signals audible to humans—trumpets, roars, screams, snorts, and rumbles—but in recent years researchers have learned that elephants also communicate with calls that include sounds too low for human hearing. Such low-frequency sounds are called infrasounds. Elephant infrasounds fall in the 14 to 24 hertz range and are combined with other sounds that humans can detect. (A human with very acute hearing can perceive sounds only as low as 20 hertz.) But though the infrasounds are low, they are very loud to animals with the equipment to hear them. Some elephant infrasounds are pounded out at up to 115 decibels, which is close to the decibel level of rock music. The sounds are powerful enough for a human to feel if standing near a vocalizing elephant, even if they are below the level of hearing. Such sounds are less affected by vegetation than higher sounds and, in theory at least, could travel for 6 miles, perhaps even farther.

Infrasound communication explains how elephants separated by several miles are able to coordinate their activities, a mystery first observed by early hunters. Biologist Rowan Martin, who studied elephants in Zimbabwe, found that families from different clans would change their course to avoid one another when traveling, even though they were miles apart and the wind did not allow them to smell one another. Presumably they heard one another across the miles. Musth bulls, too, apparently avoid coming near one another in the same way. In a sense, because infrasound allows elephants to communicate across long distances, it becomes difficult to determine whether a solitary elephant is really alone. The seemingly isolated animal might in fact be in constant

$\mathbf{W}$hile eating, a sub-adult vigorously flaps his ears—which contain many surface veins that radiate body heat—to help control his temperature.

contact with others of its social group even though they are miles away.

Studies by Joyce Poole have singled out a number of different low-frequency calls or rumbles. One is the *greeting rumble*, a loud call that elephants of the same bond group use when meeting after a separation of several hours. Longer separations are marked by more intensive greeting that involves loud rumbles, screams, trumpeting, urinating and defecating (presumably conveying some olfactory signal), and physical contact.

The *contact call*, which like many calls contains elements that humans can hear, is nearly always used by members of the same bond group. While making the call, the vocalizing elephant flaps its ears steadily. When it finishes the signal, it raises its head and spreads its ears, looking from side to side as if listening for a response. The *contact answer* sounds more abrupt and loud to human ears, softening toward the end. The answering elephant usually raises its head and ears first, apparently in response to the contact call. Field studies have shown that elephants separated by a mile or two will repeatedly call and answer, apparently locating one another even though out of sight.

Elephants also use another rumble that seems to mean "let's go." This occurs when a group is stationary, as when feeding or resting. One individual may move to the edge of the group and issue a long, unmodulated, soft rumble. At the same time, the elephant usually flaps its ears steadily and stands with one leg raised. The raised leg may itself be an *intention movement*, a physical sign that the animal wants to move on. The call may have to be repeated several times, but it usually will cause the rest of the group to move off together.

Musth males issue low, pulsated rumbles that are preceded by a folding and then waving of the ears and often followed by a loud ear flap. This might help to attract females. Females whose group has been joined by a musth bull often answer his rumbles with a *female chorus*. This low-frequency, modulated rumble is also given when females are investigated by a musth bull and when females encounter the scent of urine from a musth male.

Females also utter a *post-copulatory sequence* of rumbles, loud calls that may be repeated for up to half an hour at a diminishing rate. The sequence usually follows mating. Other females usually tend to crowd around the mated female, rumbling, trumpeting, and screaming, their temporal glands oozing as they urinate and defecate. Poole has labeled this ritual *mating pandemonium*.

As if on signal, and in fact very likely following an infrasonic warning rumble, a group of elephants in Tsavo East National Park takes flight with tails high and strides long—visual signals of panic.

The various calls are critical to elephant social life. They serve an important adaptive function. Musth bulls, for example, call much more frequently when alone and apparently in search of females than they do after they have joined a group. They often listen before uttering their calls, a sign that they may be answering or seeking other elephants. The post-copulatory call may signal that a female is at the height of estrus and may serve to attract the oldest, finest breeding males. The post-copulatory calls may be one important signal by which the bulls locate cows at the peak of estrus. The contact calls and answers and similar calls help to coordinate herd movements and to keep herds together.

Doubtless other calls remain to be discovered. Indirect and chilling, evidence for this exists. One example concerns about 80 elephants that lived in a private sanctuary in Zimbabwe. The sanctuary was adjacent to a national park, but generally the elephants stayed on the sanctuary near a game lodge where they were quite familiar with and comfortable around tourists. Sanctuary guides knew the elephants well and could find them quite easily. One day the national park started an elephant culling operation. Whole herds, in the usual way, were gunned down within seconds. On the day the cull began, the sanctuary elephants, though some 40 miles from the cull site, vanished from their usual haunts. They were later found huddled in a corner of the sanctuary as far as possible from the national park boundary. Apparently they had received an alarm of some sort from the elephants that were under attack so many miles away.

▮ ELEPHANTS AND DEATH

Several seemingly mythical stories about elephants and death have circulated for many years. One is the legend of the elephant graveyard, a hidden place to which all elephants go to die. Another is the tale that elephants will linger by their dead as if obsessed with the bones and corpses of their kind. Third are the stories about elephants sometimes burying their dead.

The first of these, about the elephant graveyard, is indeed myth. No evidence for such a place has ever been found, though this old legend has long persisted. There is something charming about the idea of an elephant graveyard; losing it to the hard reality is a bit of a letdown. It is therefore doubly captivating to learn that the other two stories—about obsession with the dead and burial—are true.

Many field observers have watched elephants milling around another's corpse. The behavior is particularly pronounced when a family witnesses the death of one of its members. Survivors will try to get the dead animal on its feet, using their tusks to lift the cadaver. They will paw at it and smell it and touch it with their trunks. Sometimes elephants will linger for days by a dead relative. Mothers whose calves die have been known to stay with their dead babies for days. Iain Douglas-Hamilton in his account of the early years of his field research tells of a cow that carried her decomposing calf on her tusks for several days.

It is not clear whether any of this means that elephants understand or have a concept of death. They may be merely responding to the inertia of an animal they care about. It is well known that elephants will help an injured relative. They often cluster around

A youngster sinks slowly into the turf as it feeds at a swamp's edge.

A young adult gets a grip on a palm frond before tearing it from its stem.

A bull blows dirt into his mouth (below) after wetting himself down at a Tsavo East watering hole. Elephants eat dirt for the mineral content, including salt. The soil passes through the digestive tract and is expelled with dung. Elephant dung on a Tsavo East National Park road is laced with dirt.

a wounded individual and press against it to keep it from falling. They also help fallen friends get back on their feet. Tending to sick and injured family members, which are nearly always relatives, benefits not only the sick animal but also the family itself. If the ministrations help an elephant to survive that would have perished by itself then the recovered individual may in turn help other herd members. Just by surviving to reproduce again, it helps ensure the genetic survival of the herd. In addition, it may also help in the rearing of young belonging to other elephants. Thus a strong desire to help injured comrades could be highly adaptive for elephants. The urge to try to lift the dead may be little more than a frustrated attempt to aid an individual whose stillness, like that of a sick animal, stimulates the helping behavior.

Harder to dismiss on instinctive or inherent behavioral grounds is the elephant's fascination with elephant bones. Often when elephants encounter a bleached skeleton they will gingerly draw near and cautiously touch the bones. They sometimes pick up bones and pass them from one to another. They occasionally carry bones for hundreds of yards and show a particular interest in tusks. They will examine tusks carefully and pass them around and carry them off and sometimes smash them against trees. Elephant interest in bones and cadavers can be so intense, with the elephants crowding so closely around the remains, that the whole group cannot participate at once but must take turns. On the other hand, some groups will ignore a corpse that has fascinated other herds, as Douglas-Hamilton discovered when he moved a dead elephant into a well-traveled elephant trail.

All this adds up to an impenetrable mystery. Because elephants live partly in an olfactory world, we can only guess at what tales the dead may tell them through scent alone. Perhaps they can identify a known individual by the odors of the death site. Perhaps they are so intensely interested in tusks because tusks are the most recognizable remnant of a dead individual. Perhaps they can detect odors that tell something of how the animal died. For example, perhaps some hormonal scent of fear lingers on the remains of an elephant killed in a cull operation and serves as a warning to elephants passing by.

A still greater mystery concerning the dead is even harder to explain. It has been reported since the era of the Roman Empire that elephants bury their dead. The Latin naturalist Aelian wrote in the year 49, "An elephant will not pass by a dead elephant without casting a branch or some dust on the body." In 1607 Edward Topsell reported of elephants in *The History of Four-Footed Beasts*, "I cannot omit their care, to bury and cover the

A male wets himself down at a Tsavo East watering hole. Mud, covered by a layer of dust, protects the skin from heat and holds in moisture.

(OPPOSITE)

Two males get first dibs on a Tsavo East watering hole, where they drink and throw mud on themselves. After they finish, other members of the group move in to drink, wallow, and roll.

Amboseli elephants set aside some time for a good wallow in an oversized puddle in the road.

A young elephant wallows in Ol Turkai Arok Swamp's black mud, covering himself from trunk to tail. The swamp's name means "place of black palms."

dead carcasses of their companions, or any others of their kind; for finding them dead they pass not by them till they have lamented their common misery, by casting dust and earth on them, and also green boughs. . . . "

These sound like ignorant tales from a prescientific time. But these observations have been corroborated by modern biologists and wildlife managers. Several cases have been recorded of elephants covering with soil and vegetation the corpses of humans they have killed. In 1956 animal tracks found in a Kenya park indicated that elephants had dragged a rhino carcass and covered it with grass and branches. In another case a hunter killed a bull elephant but could not reach the corpse because others bulls surrounded it. The hunter left the scene, presuming that if he returned later the herd would have left. When he came back he found that the fatal wound in the dead animal's head had been covered with mud, and that the body was covered with soil and leaves. In a similar case, a biologist who shot a cow elephant with a drug was prevented from reviving her by the rest of the herd. When the cow died, the matriarch covered the body with grass and branches. Joyce Poole also says that elephants often come to her camp at night and remove elephant jaws she has collected.

Iain Douglas-Hamilton in *Among the Elephants,* related a fascinating second-hand story of elephants and death: "A curious variation of the elephant's interest in bones is related by George Adamson in his book *Bwana Game.* He was obliged to shoot one of a party of bull elephants who had chased the District Commissioner around his own garden. The bull was shot at the scene of his misdemeanor, and after allowing the local Turkana tribesman to cut off as much meat as they could, Adamson had the carcass dragged about half a mile away. That night some elephants visited the body, picked up a shoulder blade and a leg bone and returned them to exactly the spot where the elephant had been shot. It was impossible to prove that they were his companions of the previous day but unless the replacement of the bones at the spot was a coincidence it seems that the place of death held some significance."

It is impossible, of course, to measure that significance or even to be sure of what it means. It may be that elephants do not understand death, but are troubled or saddened by the loss that death brings. As Douglas-Hamilton further explained, "Many great zoologists including Charles Darwin have thought that animals possess strong emotions and I have little doubt that when one of their number dies and the bonds of a lifetime are severed, elephants have a similar feeling to the one we call grief. Unfortu-

A sub-adult arches its trunk to feed or drink in Amboseli's Ol Turkai Arok Swamp.

nately science as yet has no means of measuring or describing emotion even for human beings, let alone for animals."

Nevertheless one account related by Richard Garstang, formerly a biologist with a South African national park, provides a chilling sense of what elephants may know and understand. A government hunter told him that when helicopters approach elephant herds during culls, the older animals often stand out in the open after leaving their young under the shelter of trees. "It's as if they're saying, 'take us, but leave the young alone,' Garstang said. As a biologist, Garstang said, he is trained not to attribute human qualities to animals. But speaking as a nonbiologist, he said it seems that the elephants know when the helicopters arrive that their time has come.

Nerves on edge: elephants gather close together and raise their trunks to test the air in response to danger. Their only defenses are fighting and fleeing.

Though we probably will never know precisely how elephants relate to death, one thing is certain. In recent years death has become a constant companion of Africa's elephants. The killing of African elephants has reached unprecedented levels since the early 1970s. Because elephants breed slowly—cows are not likely to give birth until more than 12 years old and then are likely to calve no more than every four years—they cannot recover quickly from heavy slaughter. In recent years the slaughter increased, and elephant numbers declined persistently. If the death rates of the last few years had continued, the African elephant probably would have become extinct within the next 15 years.

AFRICA FIGHTS
TO SAVE
ITS ELEPHANTS

"We shall let life run easily here! Just sit still and gather in the ivory those savages will bring. This country has its good points, after all!"

Joseph Conrad, "An Outpost of Progress" in *Tales of Unrest*

∎

Elephants used to roam in great herds over all the more woody districts, but have now been quite driven out of Cape Colony, Natal, and the two Dutch republics. . . . From these regions he will soon vanish, and unless something is done to stop the hunting of elephants the total extinction of the animals in Africa may be expected within another half-century; for the foolish passion for slaughter which sends so-called sportsmen on his track, and the high price of ivory, are lessening his numbers day by day.

James Bryce, *Impressions of South Africa*, 1900

∎

Owing to the constant persecution for the sake of its tusks, the African elephant has been greatly reduced in numbers, and is now practically exterminated from large areas in the southern portion of the continent. Indeed, if measures are not shortly taken for its protection, it stands a good chance of sharing the fate which has already befallen the quagga and Burchell's rhinoceros.

Richard Lydekker, *The Royal Natural History*, 1894

∎

The other day I was talking with a good friend to whom all hunting is dull except elephant hunting. To him there is no sport in anything unless there is great danger and, if the danger is not enough, he will increase it for his own satisfaction. A hunting companion of his had told me how this friend was not satisfied with the risks of ordinary elephant hunting but would, if possible, have the elephants driven, or turned, so he could take them head on, so it was a choice of killing them with the difficult frontal shot as they came, trumpeting, with their ears spread, or having them run over him.

Ernest Hemingway, *By-Line: Ernest Hemingway*

∎

To me the death of an elephant is one of the saddest sights in the world.

Iain Douglas-Hamilton, *Among the Elephants*

∎

ON JULY 17, 1989, MORE THAN 13 TONS OF ELEphant tusks were stacked some 30 feet high on the sunswept plains of Nairobi National Park. The tusks lay on huge logs cut from olive and gum trees, forming a massive, jagged mountain of ivory. The tusks came in all sizes. Some you could hold in one hand; others, thrust upright into the ground, would tower over anyone who stood beside them. All were marked with black numbers for official identification.

Game rangers and policemen milled around the vast pile as a crowd slowly gathered in the early afternoon. All watched while two men poured countless gallons of gasoline over the tusks, as if anointing the ivory for some strange ritual. As, in a way, they were.

About 50 yards from the tusks, twenty drums of fuel rested beneath a tree. A pump stood near the drums and a pipe stretched from the pump to the stack and on under the tusks. Everything was ready. Within moments the pump could be turned on and gasoline could be sent down the pipe and up into the stack of tusks.

In mid-afternoon, ministers of the government and members of the Kenyan parliament arrived, followed shortly by a motorcade that marked the arrival of Daniel arap Moi, the president of Kenya. Moi strode to a podium set up to receive him and gave a short speech. Among his remarks was this: "Great objectives require great sacrifices. I now call upon the people of the world to join us in Kenya by eliminating the trade in ivory once and for all."

Shortly, he left the podium and walked to the mountain of tusks. The crowd surged forward, closing around him. Within moments Moi had put flame to the tusks. Black smoke billowed into the sky, and the crowd cheered. By early evening the 13 tons of tusks were reduced to ashes.

In July 1989 Kenyan President Daniel arap Moi set fire to 13 tons of elephant tusks confiscated from poachers. It was a symbolic event. Moi showed that Kenya would no longer tolerate the butchering of elephants for the sake of profit.

Tusks stacked 30 feet high are (OPPOSITE) reduced to ashes by the flames set in motion by President Moi. Elephants, along with rhinos, are the foundation of Kenya's half-billion-dollar annual tourist trade. If poachers wipe out the animals, Kenya's economy will suffer. Moi burned the tusks to help save elephants by drawing world attention to the animals' troubles. During a speech at the burn he said, "Great objectives require great sacrifices. I now call upon the people of the world to join us in Kenya by eliminating the trade in ivory once and for all."

The ivory that was burned on that July day had been confiscated from poachers who had slaughtered thousands of elephants to get it. The ivory's destruction was a symbolic gesture on the part of Daniel arap Moi. He was saying that Kenya would no longer tolerate the butchering of elephants for the sake of profit, that trade in the nation's ivory must stop. This was a turning point in the history of the ivory trade, perhaps even a landmark in the history of humanity's relationship to the elephant.

The ivory trade has long been a threat to the elephant and in the past 10 years has wiped out more than half of those remaining in Africa. For individual nations the problem is much worse. In those same years, the ivory trade claimed more than 90 percent of the elephants living on unprotected lands in Kenya and 70 percent of those on protected lands, such as national parks. For many years the slaughter received the tacit approval of the government, but under Moi that has changed, as the burning of the ivory showed. For the first time ever, the elephant's survival was being placed ahead of immediate monetary gain.

The symbolic importance of those flames cannot be overestimated. The ivory that was reduced to ashes was valued at some

Ivory carvings on sale in a New York City shop. Until the ivory trade was banned, the United States provided the market for about a third of the world's supply of carved ivory.

The world's largest land mammal has been killed by the hundreds of thousands to supply such products as elephant-foot tables and carved ivory souvenirs.

Richard E. Leakey, head of Kenya's Wildlife Services, proposed President Daniel arap Moi's well-publicized burning of $3 million in confiscated ivory. This monument was erected in Nairobi National Park to commemorate the event. Leakey, after assuming office in 1989, boosted the budget for Kenya's wildlife law enforcement officers, acquired better arms, and organized vigilant park patrols. Combined with Moi's shoot-to-kill order against poachers and an international ban on ivory trade, Leakey's measures have helped cut poaching in Kenya.

$3 million, and its destruction was indeed a great sacrifice for Kenya, where the average person earns only $20 a month. But Kenya and other African nations are facing a new era in which values are changing. Tourism is Kenya's biggest source of foreign exchange, bringing in about $500 million yearly. Surveys show that most tourists come to see wildlife, particularly elephants and rhinos, two of the most heavily poached species. If Kenya should lose its elephants, it may well lose the bulk of its income. A survey of safari operators and tourists in Kenya showed that elephants

Caution! Slow-moving traffic. A bull elephant rewrites the rules of the road, drawing tour buses from miles away. Elephants are among the most popular park attractions, along with rhinos and big cats.

bring in an estimated $200 million yearly. A living elephant is worth about $14,375 a year to Kenya for every year of its life, giving it a potential value of nearly $900,000. The ivory of a dead elephant is worth less than $1,000, and if the animal is taken by poachers, none of that money helps the Kenyan economy. Never before have living elephants been so important to a human society.

■ BLOOD AND IVORY: THE SELLING OF A SPECIES

Trade in elephant products was already well under way at the dawn of history. Four tusks were found among the remains of the palace at Zacro, on eastern Crete, which was destroyed about 1,450 B.C. An ivory shop dating from the same period was found at Cnossus. Among the artifacts were large statuettes whose parts were carved from ivory and assembled with pins and dowels. The Mycenaeans carved statues from ivory and produced a variety of ivory luxury items, such as boxes, combs, and seals. By the ninth century, ivory was widely used in the Greek world. The Egyptian pharoahs brought ivory up from Sudan, and the Persian king Darius left an inscription in stone in which he boasted that construction of his palace required ivory from, among other places, faraway Kush, now called Ethiopia. By 350 B.C. the Greeks were draining Libya and other north African nations of ivory. The Phoenicians traded widely in ivory, some of which came from Ethiopia and Somalia.

The Roman Empire created the first excessive demand for ivory. In the first century after Christ, the opulence of Rome created a shortage in ivory supplies from Africa. Trade continued in later centuries, doubtless contributing to, and perhaps causing, the eventual extinction of north Africa's elephants in the seventh century. As trade in ivory from north Africa collapsed, Rome turned to other sources, building up the ivory trade in Ethiopia and Somalia.

Ivory in the ancient world, as in today's, was a symbol of wealth and status. In the shadowed halls of royal tombs lie great numbers of ivory artifacts. King Solomon bought vast quantities of ivory for the building of his palace in 1,000 B.C. and had an entire throne made of ivory plated with gold. In the Roman era, ivory was used for bird cages, scabbards, brooches, combs, scepters, bookcovers, musical instruments, chariots, even doors and floors. Cicero wrote of rich houses that glittered with ivory.

The Mediterranean world was not alone in its passion for ivory. The ivory trade grew rich and fat in Arabia as well. The Arabians were among the first traders to penetrate east Africa in search of tusks, and by the tenth century had established trading centers and colonies on east Africa's coasts and islands. Most of the ivory in the Arab trade was sent to China, though small amounts trickled into medieval Europe. European desire for more ivory drove the Portuguese to explore Africa in the fifteenth and sixteenth centuries. As a result, tons of ivory began reaching Europe, a trade that continued even when Portugal lost its influence in subsequent centuries.

The real boom in the ivory trade came in the nineteenth century. Two factors created the boom. The more important of these was the sudden wealth that the Industrial Revolution brought to

Vultures roost and a monkey plays in the branches of an acacia tree as dusk falls over Amboseli National Park, one of Kenya's few safe havens for elephants.

Europe and America. In the tradition of earlier peoples, the new rich were ravenous for the trappings of wealth, and among the foremost of these glittering possessions was ivory. Ivory was used for buttons, brush handles, letter openers, figurines, fans, card cases, and other luxury items. It was also a critical ingredient in two new fad items that no Victorian trendsetter could do without—billiard balls for the then-fashionable parlor game and keys for the pianos that were socially important symbols of wealth and culture. Tens of thousands of elephants died for the sake of Victorian social status.

The second factor was the existence of well-established trade routes. These had been carved into the African interior primarily by Arab merchants who opened the continent for a burgeoning ivory trade. In addition Arab merchants and colonies were already on hand to administer the trade and force upon it some sort of order.

The nineteenth century trade in ivory helped create the white hunters, Europeans who combined sport and profit by slaughtering elephants for tusks. Despite the blood shed by the white hunters and the brutality many showed to their native workers, the adventurer/hunters represented the kinder side of the ivory trade. In the early era, Arab traders created personal fiefdoms and ruled with horrifying duplicity and brutality.

Modern trade began with Said ibn Sultan, the ruler of Oman and of all of Africa's Arab settlement. In 1840 he established his capital on the island of Zanzibar and created a clove industry there and on the island of Pemba. When he invited the leading western nations to trade in the harbor at Zanzibar, one item much in demand was ivory. So it was in search of ivory that Said sent caravans deep into Africa.

Said was not interested in ivory alone. He was also in search of slaves for his clove plantations. But the two interests were not separate and distinct. The ivory trade would have been impossible without slaves to transport the ivory from the interior to Zanzibar, and thousands of Africans were eventually shackled into the misery of the ivory business.

The Arabs considered ivory of far more importance than slaves, who generally were captured from enemy tribes by native allies of the Arabs and provided to the ivory dealers as cheap beasts of burden. The Arabs' main interest was getting the ivory home. Surviving slaves, turned into a tidy little profit in the slave markets at Zanzibar, were merely a bonus. Consequently the Arabs treated the slaves with unimaginable barbarity. The slaves were forced to carry tusks, many weighing in excess of 100 pounds, for more than a thousand miles. They were often chained together by their necks or, worse, had their necks locked into a *gorree*, a pole about 6 feet long with forked ends. The neck was locked into the fork with a metal bar fixed so that if the slave fell the wrong way or struggled the neck might break. To keep the exhausted slaves moving, guards armed with rifles, knives, and spears beat them with whips. One British observer wrote that the whips were used so liberally that in many of the slaves the "feet and shoulders were a mass of open sores, made more painful by the swarms of flies which followed the march and lived on the flowing blood." Women, who equalled the enslaved men in number, usually carried babies on their backs and tusks on their heads.

Native bearers, probably enslaved by elephant hunters, carry a burdern of ivory to market in this drawing by Thure de Thulstrup that was published in *Harper's* in 1888. The ivory trade was the foundation of commerce in slaves, since slaves were needed to carry tusks for hundreds of miles from killing grounds to markets.

If a woman became too fatigued to carry both, the baby was killed. "We cannot leave valuable ivory on the road," one guard said. "We spear the child and make the burden lighter. Ivory first, child afterwards." Any male slave who fell by the wayside was killed with an axe. This prevented slaves from feining exhaustion in an attempt to escape.

The ivory trade had a vast effect on the native peoples, even among tribes whose military power or access to ivory kept them free of slavery. As the natives came to understand how much wealth could be made by trading ivory, their social structure was shattered. Chiefs abandoned their people to organize safaris, leaving themselves vulnerable to rivals and their subjects vulnerable to enemy tribes. The problem of lost leadership was compounded by the loss of warriors who joined ivory caravans as porters, guides, and hunters, leaving their homes defenseless for months and even years. Firearms, provided to favored native peoples in return for ivory, pervaded Africa, spurring and intensifying native warfare and speeding the destruction of wildlife. Social and political groups fell apart as they divided into rival factions—the tra-

ditionalists who wanted to maintain the old values and the icon-
oclasts who wanted to participate in the ivory craze.

The ivory trade shaped the life and future of one man in particular, and he as a result shaped much of Africa. This was Hamed
bin Muhammad el Murjebi, better known as Tippu Tip, a nick-
name that meant "the blinker," a reference to a nervous twitching
of his eyelids. He was a descendent of one of the first Zanzibari
Arabs to blaze a trail into interior Africa. By arming some native
peoples so they could defeat and enslave enemy tribes, he built
up a system of alliances that eventually made him the virtual ruler
of some 250,000 square miles of east and central Africa, from Lake
Tanganyika in the east to the Lubilash River in the west, from
central Lualaba in the north to Katanga in the south. He made and
broke chiefs, made and ended wars, set the price of ivory, and
controlled the ivory trade. He was instrumental in helping many
European explorers whose expeditions would have ended in tragedy without his aid.

One who owed Tippu Tip much of his fame, if not his life as
well, was Henry Stanley, the man who tracked down David Livingstone and uttered the immortal phrase, "Doctor Livingstone, I
presume." After discovering Livingstone in east Africa, Stanley
went on in 1876 to try to discover whether the Lualaba River was
part of the Nile or the Congo river system. Stanley traveled with
Tippu Tip for two months through the Congo rainforests, a region
dreaded by native peoples because of the harshness of its swamps,
the deadliness of the diseases that could be contracted there, and
the hostility of forest natives. The presence of Tippu Tip and a
few hundred of his men helped ensure that Stanley would not
readily fall victim to native hostility, but even Tippu Tip's influence was useless against disease. Scores of his men died of small-
pox before the Arab parted ways with Stanley, who went on to
travel the length of the Congo. Tippu Tip received ample reward
for his tribulations, though. During the journey he found fertile
new elephant grounds and native peoples whose interest in ivory
was so scant that they used tusks as buttresses in their houses. He
was able to trade for ivory at a profit of about $50 for each dollar
he spent.

Tippu Tip remained in power until the end of the nineteenth
century. He was unique in the tremendous authority, wealth, and
influence that he wielded, but he was not unusual in his pursuit
of ivory. Thousands of people were joining the ivory trade, bringing guns and death into elephant country. Khartoum, a city in
Sudan at the confluence of the White and Blue Niles, became another capital of the ivory trade, feeding tusks not to Zanzibar, but

A nineteenth century ivory market in Addis Ababa, Abyssinia. The ivory trade boomed in the 1800s as Europe and the United States profited from the Industrial Revolution. Trendsetters and social climbers were the biggest consumers of ivory products, especially billiard balls and piano keys. Elephant populations declined precipitously as hunters killed them without limit.

(OPPOSITE)
The massive tusks on this big bull are critical to its survival, since it uses them for a variety of important tasks. The tusks are also an open invitation to poachers. Says Oria Douglas-Hamilton, "tusk are both the life and the death of the elephants."

down the Nile to Cairo, which became another important trade depot. Toward the end of the nineteenth century, Khartoum was an international city swarming with adventurers, an ivory boom town that served as a gateway to the interior. From Khartoum traveled the hunters who opened the upper Nile to exploration, who reached the edges of the Congo rainforest, who first brought European influence to the place that would one day be called Uganda. They traded with native peoples for ivory, giving 4 or 5 pounds of colored beads, 200 or 300 cowie shells, and perhaps half a dozen copper bracelets for a 100-pound tusk.

The trade was peaceful and even amiable until the natives had their fill of beads, and the elephants had been wiped out in the easily reached areas around the Nile. Then began the usual cycle of pillaging and enslavement as hunters formed armies, attacked and burned native villages, killed the men, enslaved the women and children, and stole any ivory they found. Hunters, in the pattern that worked so well for Tippu Tip, formed alliances with

some tribes and helped them destroy their enemies. The hunters gave the tribes stolen cattle and enslaved enemy women in return for tusks. Men who organized ivory-trading forays would pay their porters and other help by giving them slaves. The practice was carefully hidden in account books by listing payment in terms of the dollar-value of the slaves, making it appear that the porters were paid in cash or in goods such as soap, shoes, and cloth. A foray involving 150 men could bring in 20,000 pounds of ivory worth 4,000 pounds sterling. Since porters and other help were paid by giving them slaves, there was no overhead for wages. Usually the ivory trader was left with a surplus of 400 or 500 slaves, whose sale added to his profit.

Despite the activity of European hunters based in Khartoum, Arab traders, with Tippu Tip the most powerful among them, controlled the bulk of the ivory trade until the end of the nineteenth century. Then the advance of European conquest shifted the balance of power. Germany, England, France, Belgium, and the rest of the imperialist league divided Africa among them. By then the elephant was in serious decline throughout most of sub-Saharan Africa. In the 1880s and 1890s, the elephants of Kenya and Uganda were being hunted down ruthlessly for their ivory. The effect on the elephants was obvious to keen observers. Joseph Thomson, leading a Royal Geographical Society expedition in 1879 to the area surrounding Lake Victoria, wrote that though ivory hunters treated elephants as if they were inexhaustible, they were not. "Nothing could be more absurd. Let me simply mention a fact. In my sojourn of fourteen months, during which I passed over an immense area of the Great Lakes region, *I never once saw a single elephant.* Twenty years ago they roamed over those countries unmolested, and now they have been almost utterly exterminated."

The European governments that ruled Africa at the turn of the century attempted to put some controls on hunting and to establish game reserves. But they were also committed financially to hunting. Ivory could be counted on to bring some 4,500 pounds yearly to British East Africa, as Kenya was called, and the money could be used for such purposes as building a railway across the nation. Customs on private trade in ivory brought in additional money.

But the elephant could not withstand the slaughter. By 1900 both British and German East Africa had enacted strict controls on elephant hunting. However, game laws were poorly enforced until 1910, and even then were not completely effective. On the eve of World War I, no less than 50,000 elephants were being slaughtered each year for the ivory trade, with no end in sight.

▮ ELEPHANT PROTECTION

The first effort to protect the African elephant began in 1884, when Paul Kruger urged the parliament of the Transvaal Republic to establish national reserves for wildlife protection. Four years later he shepherded through parliament a resolution calling for parks in which wildlife and their habitat would be preserved in a pristine condition, but it was not until 1894 that he succeeded in establishing Africa's first wildlife sanctuary, the Pongola Reserve. The following year the government created the Sabi and Shingwedzie game reserves. In 1902 a hunter named James Stevenson-Hamilton was made a full-time game warden at Sabi. In 1926 Sabi and Shingwedzie were combined with land that lay between into a 7,000-square-mile reserve appropriately dubbed Kruger National Park.

Southern Africa led the continent in establishing game reserves, and the benefits of adequate protection soon paid off. In

A bloated cadaver is mute testimony to the poachers' work. In many parts of Africa, the remains of dead elephants outnumber living animals.

1895 only 10 elephants remained in what would be Kruger National Park, but today the park is said to have as many elephants as it can hold. It is one of the parks where elephants are culled periodically. Given good protection, elephants are able to rebound.

The first nation to follow in the footsteps of the Transvaal Republic was Tanzania, which created the Kilimanjaro and Selous reserves in 1914. The idea of protecting wildlife habitat caught on slowly. It was not until the 1940s and 1950s that other nations began quickly to create parks and reserves. But by then the pendulum clearly had swung from wildlife exploitation to wildlife protection—in those two decades at least 13 parks were created across Africa.

Despite the new laws and parks, ivory hunting continued. It could not possibly end as long as the consumers of Europe, the United States, and the Orient demanded ivory products. Poachers supplied the markets, evading the few law enforcement officers and moving their operations from nation to nation depending upon which government was cracking down on poachers and which was giving up the effort. Poaching affected all wildlife, since the poachers had to live off the land, killing antelope and other animals for meat as they hunted for elephants. They also had devastating effects on elephants, since they ignored laws that protected elephant cows and offspring.

Elephants were being assaulted not only by European ivory hunters but also by native poachers. The establishment of parks almost always displaced native peoples from at least some of their lands. They resented the parks and resented being told that they could no longer hunt the game they had pursued since time beyond memory. At the same time, ivory traders offered them money, alcohol, firearms, and drugs in return for ivory. Resentment of the new restrictions, coupled with the enticements of the ivory traders, compelled native peoples in many areas to poach elephants. Had they continued hunting elephants at traditional levels, the effect on the populations probably would have been slight. But as they turned from hunting for meat to hunting for money, the number of animals they killed escalated. In Kenya's Tsavo National Park, one group of local poachers killed 7,000 elephants in the 1950s within little more than two years. Had they been hunting only for food, the local hunters might not have killed this number of elephants in the course of two centuries or more.

Although elephants in many parks were under assault by poachers, in some areas their numbers were also increasing under

the new protective regimes. Moreover, farms were spreading out into elephant territory and abutting parks. This combination created new problems. As elephants found old feeding grounds converted to agriculture, they simply ate the crops. Colonial governments during the 1930s, 40s, and 50s often responded by killing the offending elephants. In some districts of Tanzania, efforts were even made to exterminate the animals. About the only place where elephants were safe from crop protection was on parks and reserves. Game rangers often patrolled park borders, killing elephants that, following ancient drives and patterns of movement, left the parks for other feeding grounds when food sources were scarce. The elephants were thus imprisoned in the parks, where they often were victims of poachers.

The mother of a week-old calf feeds with her family on the outskirts of Ol Turkai Swamp. Poachers have killed off vast numbers of herd matriarchs and mothers. At Manyara only three of 125 females alive in 1965 survived to the end of the 1980s. The leadership of elder cows, so important to elephant life, has been destroyed. Females barely old enough to have their first calves are now leading entire herds of orphans.

The ivory trade escalated after the fall of the colonial governments in the 1960s and 1970s. Even in nations that ostensibly protected their elephants, poaching sometimes received official sanction. In Kenya, which banned hunting in 1977, elephants were reduced from 70,000 animals in 1973 to perhaps half that number 10 years later. Kenya's biggest dealer in illegal ivory at that time was the United African Corporation, which was chaired by Margaret Kenyatta, who was the mayor of Nairobi and the daughter of Kenyan president Jomo Kenyatta. Records show that in 1975 Kenya exported to Hong Kong at least 46 tons of illegal ivory valued at about $2 million. The Kenyatta family grew rich on the slaughter of their nation's elephants.

In 1979 Iain Douglas-Hamilton completed a survey of elephant populations in Africa and concluded that about 1.3 million elephants still roamed there. But his data would soon be hopelessly out of date. The price of ivory was on the rise, and with it the killing of elephants reached new heights.

The price of ivory had been stable at about $2.50 a pound until the late 1960s. Then ivory became popular as a form of hard currency, like gold—a material that could be hoarded as a hedge against inflation. By 1973 raw ivory was selling for $14 a pound. Five years later the price had nearly tripled. It soared further in the 1980s, hitting $114 in Oriental markets in 1989. Poachers make only a fraction of that amount, perhaps $6 a pound. But that is still a compelling price, since even at that rate an African poacher can make the equivalent of a year's wages by killing just two elephants. As prices rose the killing intensified. Today, the elephant slaughter even bears political overtones. Tourism is Kenya's greatest source of foreign dollars, and the foundation of that industry is elephants and rhinos. These are the creatures that bring in the tourists. Somalia, which borders Kenya on the north, permits elephant poachers to set up camps in Somalia, from which the poachers make raids into Kenya. Somali officials thus are helping to weaken Kenya by undercutting its economy. Strikes against Kenya's wildlife even bear the trappings of open warfare—uniformed Somali soldiers sometimes make raids into Kenya to kill elephants and rhinos.

The killing of elephants in the 1970s and 1980s was driven by many social and political events. Many African governments were unstable and could not protect wildlife. Fluctuating oil prices and widespread inflation drove local investors to seek a stable home for their money, and ivory was a sound investment. Elephants had increased in many areas because of protection in earlier years, and human populations had risen, pushing humans and elephants

In Tsavo National Park, elephants with tusks as big as this bull's are a rare sight. Tsavo is the most heavily poached park in Kenya because its size—some 8,000 square miles— makes it difficult to patrol and because its location provides easy access to the sea and neighboring nations.

together. Vast quantities of firearms had flooded into Africa. African arms imports increased ten-fold in the 1970s, and armed forces tripled in east Africa. When arms and armies increase in Africa, wildlife poaching escalates too.

Between 1980 and 1987, poachers destroyed more than half the continent's elephant population, reducing the 1.3 million to perhaps 600,000. The damage caused by the slaughter was compounded because the elephants with the biggest tusks—the bulls—were killed first. As the big tuskers were killed off, poachers turned their guns on the smaller cows and even on calves with tiny tusks. Consequently the slaughter escalated as more elephants were killed to keep the tonnage of Africa's ivory export at the same yearly level. In 1979, Hong Kong, one of the leading ivory markets, imported 521 tons of ivory, representing the deaths of 31,000 elephants. In 1988, only 290 tons were imported, but because average tusk size had shrunk from about 20 pounds to about 10 pounds, that tonnage represented at least 33,000 dead elephants.

The slaughter wiped out astounding numbers of elephants in the 1980s. Kenya lost 85 percent of its elephants and Tanzania lost 22,000 elephants a year during that decade. Naftali S. Gwae, a law enforcement officer in Tanzania, said that the 3,000 elephants that roamed Serengeti National Park were reduced to 450 within six years. Less than half of the 109,000 elephants that lived in Tanzania's Selous Game Reserve in 1976 survived the next decade, and by the end of that decade those survivors had been reduced to about 30,000. Chad's 15,000 elephants were cut to 2,000. Poachers equipped with machetes for hacking ivory from the faces of elephants and armed with automatic weapons supplied by ivory dealers nearly wiped out the elephants of southern Sudan. A recent aerial survey of Somalia tallied more dead than living elephants. The 90,000 elephants that lived in the Central African Republic in 1976 were cut to perhaps 15,000 nine years later.

One measure of the extent of the slaughter was the rise of poaching in the rainforests of central Africa. By the end of the 1980s, poaching was reaching from the main arena, Africa's easily traveled and hunted savannas, into the more difficult forest terrain. As bush elephants dwindled, the elusive forest elephants were expected to provide the next ivory mother lode. In Cameroon, Pygmies who had hunted elephants for centuries with bows and poisoned arrows were being armed with rifles and commissioned to use their formidable skills in behalf of the ivory trade. Poaching was increasing in the Congo as new roads were cut into

A female, having slapped some black mud onto her back and head, strides across Ol Turkai Arok Swamp. Because poachers prize large tusks, which bring more money per pound, they seek out the largest elephants—the bulls and older matriarchs. This means the herds suffer not only long-term biological losses through elimination of the strongest and largest animals, but also the loss of vital social and ecological knowledge gained by the animals through years of experience.

Contact among elephants helps reinforce social bonds. Here elephants exchange friendly greetings, during which an accidental tusk-poke goes politely unacknowledged. Poaching has killed off so many of the animals that the social fabric of elephant life has been torn asunder. In many areas bewildered juveniles are forced to fend for themselves after poachers kill their elders.

the forest, often by oil companies. During the 1970s, about 200 elephants a day were killed in Zaire. Data from Zaire is scarce, but in 1990 experts believed the killing had not slowed. Some evidence suggested that Zaire government officials were involved in the illegal ivory trade.

The slaughter has left scarcely any east and central African elephant population, or even individual herd, unscathed and has had immense effects on elephant social structure. Among the several hundred Lake Manyara elephants studied by Iain Douglas-Hamilton in the late 1960s and early 1970s, few over 30 years old survived the 1980s. All across Africa bulls have been particularly hard hit. A 1988 survey of Tanzania's Mkomazi game preserve found no adult bulls, though mature bulls had constituted half the park's elephant population 20 years earlier. An aerial census the following year found no elephants in Mkomazi.

A keeper of an orphan elephant feeds his charge at David Sheldrick Wildlife Trust in Nairobi National Park. The organization receives many babies orphaned by poachers. Contact is important to motherless calves; each orphan establishes a favorite hold on its keeper before drinking. The formula is a special mixture containing coconut oil, with glucose, vitamin C, calcium, minerals, and salt added. Keepers stay with the orphans constantly, even sleeping with them to prevent the motherless calves from feeling abandoned. Most of the orphans lost their families through poaching, arriving at the trust in a state of shock and depression.

Vodka bottles hold the orphan elephants' formula, a special mixture for sensitive human babies, devoid of cow-milk fat, which the calves cannot assimilate. The orphans are milk-dependent for the first 18 months of life. The calves are fed in three-hour intervals throughout the day and night, consuming some 30 quarts daily. By age two, calves eat enough vegetation to be weaned off milk.

Calves, like human babies, comfort themselves by suckling. They will use their trunks as pacifiers or, as this orphan is doing, suck the hand that feeds them. The head of the orphan center is Daphne Sheldrick, widow of David Sheldrick, the former Tsavo National Park administrator for whom the orphan center is named. She has worked with elephants for about 30 years. Some of the orphans are being released at Tsavo, where their integration into the wild is being studied by biologist Barbara McKnight.

The mature females have also been wiped out in areas hit by poaching. Of the 125 matriarchs that lived around Lake Manyara when Douglas-Hamilton started his study, only three were alive some 20 years later in 1989. Young females, many in their teens, are trying to lead herds of orphaned babies and juveniles, a role that the teenagers would not have assumed for another 30 or 40 years had it not been for the slaughter. They lack the knowledge of terrain and of food and water supplies that the older females would have taught them. Observers say the young females lead their families as if dazed and confused. Over much of East Africa the old family structure, with females in their 40s and 50s leading family groups bred by bulls over 40, will not recover for another 20 or 30 years, and then only if the killing is stopped. The craft of survival that the old, lost elephants had passed on from generation to generation for thousands of years—the certain knowledge

A yearling orphan elephant puts his trunk into his companion's mouth, an important step in learning what plants to eat. One of the orphans, who grew up with orphan rhinos, made the mistake of putting his proboscis into a rhino's mouth and wound up with a disfigured trunk tip.

163

of where to find water in droughts, where to find food during famine, where to seek protection from enemies—has been lost, the chain of knowledge broken. It is not clear how the elephants will recover this essential knowledge, or whether they can. The effects of widespread poaching will ring through the elephant's world for decades, eroding their survival.

◼ POACHING AND THE IVORY BUSINESS

The poaching of elephants for ivory and the destruction of Africa's elephant population began in the markets of the United States, Europe, and Japan. Consumers of ivory in these nations established the demand for ivory and financed the poachers whose firepower cut down the elephants. If the elephant vanishes from Africa, the cause of its extinction will have been the ivory figurines displayed in shop windows on Fifth Avenue in New York City, the ivory signature seals with which the Japanese like to sign their names, and the ivory trinkets sold in Antwerp, London, and Paris.

At the height of the elephant slaughter, from 40 to 60 percent of all ivory was bought by Japan, nearly 500 tons yearly through

© 1989, Washington Post Writers Group. Reprinted with permission.

the mid-1980s. Nearly a third of those 500 tons were cut into *hankos*, small seals bearing an individual's personal hallmark. They are dipped in ink and used to sign checks and official documents. During the 1980s about 2 million hankos were produced yearly in Japan. The Japanese were reluctant to use hankos made from other materials because, they said, ivory carries ink better than wood or plastic and is more prestigious because it is more costly.

About a third of Africa's ivory export was shipped to the United States and Europe. In the 1980s U.S. trade in carved ivory required the deaths of an estimated 32,000 elephants yearly, ac-

The intricate beauty of this ivory statue began with the death of an elephant slain only for its tusks. At least 80 percent of the ivory traded worldwide was taken from elephants killed illegally. The slaughter demolished elephant numbers and social structure, cutting populations by half within a few years.

cording to figures compiled by TRAFFIC, a division of the World Wildlife Fund. Raw ivory, as uncarved tusks are called, accounted for perhaps 3,000 more each year, a total of 42,000 elephants annually to supply the United States with elephant products such as figurines, jewelry, and expensive footwear—luxury items all.

Though nations that claimed a surplus of elephants culled them legally until 1990 and sold their products under an international export quota system that was supposed to limit carefully the number of animals killed, fully 80 percent, perhaps even 90 percent, of the ivory that reached the markets was taken illegally from poached animals. The demand for ivory in the developed nations was met in Africa by local people working alone, by large parties of organized poachers, and by soldiers from revolutionary armies. Even official personnel were involved. One observer with years of experience in the field said that in 1988 game rangers in Kenya watched through binoculars as men wearing Kenyan military brass shot down a herd of elephants. When the rangers called upon an army base for support to stop the poachers, they were told that troops were on the way—but none ever arrived.

Poachers usually move quietly about on foot. When they kill elephants, they hack out the ivory using axes or machetes. They

The remains of an elephant killed for its tusks. The face has been hacked away to free the ivory. This has been the fate of perhaps a million elephants during the past decade.

carry the ivory to black markets or bury it in the bush for later retrieval. The poachers are the foot soldiers of the ivory trade, the men on the frontline of an increasingly intense battle between those who want to save elephants and those who want to profit from ivory. Though they take the greatest physical risks, they receive the smallest rewards—$5 or $6 a pound for ivory that may sell for 20 and even, on occasion, 40 times that in the ivory markets of Taiwan or Hong Kong.

A small percentage of the ivory exported by Africa in the 1980s was legal. Trade in legal ivory was supposed to be monitored under an international treaty, the Convention on International Trade in Endangered Species of Wild Fauna and Flora, abbreviated to CITES. More than 100 nations are signatories to the CITES agreement, which seeks to control trade in wildlife products by entering species on two lists, called appendices. No commercial trade is permitted in species listed on Appendix I. Limited, carefully monitored trade is allowed in products made from species on Appendix II.

The African elephant was listed as an Appendix II species in 1977. In 1985, CITES established the Ivory Control System to tighten international trade restrictions on ivory. Each ivory-producing nation that was a signatory to CITES was supposed to set an annual quota on the amount of ivory it would export. Under the control system, tusks were stamped with registration numbers to keep track of them. Tusks that went through the CITES system as they traveled from Africa to the importing nations were supposed to come from legal sources. If the system had worked, production of such ivory would not have hurt elephant populations.

The problem in the 1980s was that the CITES system was unworkable and poorly enforced. Indeed, CITES has *no* enforcement abilities. Each nation follows CITES rules and regulations at its own initiative. If a nation wishes to ignore a species listing, it simply registers a reservation saying it will do so. In addition, quotas and registrations often are abused, and permits often are forged or issued fraudulently. Consequently trade in illegal ivory burgeoned. Somalia, for example, declared that it would export 8,000 tusks in 1988, a year in which the nation held only 4,500 elephants, many of them young. The classic case of abuse in the 1980s was Burundi, an African nation that became a focal point of illegal ivory export. Burundi exported more than 2,000 tons of ivory from 1975 to 1988 even though the nation had no elephants. Officials claimed that the ivory had been seized from smugglers.

A big bull strides among grazing gnu and marabou storks not far from Amboseli Serena Lodge, a popular tourist spot. Each elephant, if allowed to live out its life, is worth nearly $1 million in tourist revenue. If killed for ivory, it will net less than $2,000.

Worse still was the lackluster approach of CITES officials to controlling the ivory trade. After the CITES registration process began in 1985, Burundi was permitted to register 90 tons of clearly illegal ivory. CITES justified this on the grounds that getting rid of the illegal tusks would make it easier to monitor trade in the future. Nevertheless Burundi quickly accumulated another 90 tons of ivory and, as recently as the summer of 1989, was permitted by CITES officials to register 28 tons. Legalization of poached ivory was a boon to nations such as Burundi, since illegal ivory was only worth about $25 a pound, but once legalized by CITES was worth over a $100 a pound and possibly twice that.

Ivory smuggling has been aided by various government officials. João Soares, son of Portuguese president Mario Soares, and two members of the Portuguese parliament were implicated in ivory smuggling when the small plane they were flying crashed in Angola and was reportedly found to be carrying nearly 1,000 illegal tusks among its cargo. Those caught smuggling in Tanzania included a member of the nation's parliament, who was caught with 105 illegal tusks and sentenced to 12 years in prison; Indonesia's former ambassador to Tanzania, who set up an illegal ivory carving operation in his embassy and tried to smuggle more than 200 tusks out of the country in 1989; and even a Catholic priest.

Sudan, like several other African nations, has been a major conduit for illegal ivory, and movement of ivory into and out of Sudan shows how the trade is conducted throughout Africa. In nations such as Uganda, Zaire, and the Central African Republic, tusks are loaded onto donkeys, horses, and camels and taken to collection points in southern Sudan, where poachers have already wiped out virtually all elephants. The tusks are then carried across Sudan in cargo trucks, personal luggage, and shipping crates, making their way to airports in the south. From there they are flown into northern Sudan or to import nations. The caravan routes into southern Sudan are limited in number and well known, so they could be targeted for control. Moreover, the local anti-poaching unit, the Equatorial Wildlife Conservation and National Parks Forces, has firearms equal to those of the poachers and the will to fight. But because the authorities lack good transportation and communications equipment, they often arrive too late at the scenes of poaching operations.

Although some poachers are lone gunmen hunting with antiquated weapons, many more are well-equipped and organized like military units. Using fully automatic weapons, such as an AK-47 assault rifle that can fire 360 rounds a minute, they can quickly bring down whole family groups. They can also combat

Trunks held high to sense danger on the wind, an elephant herd bunches together in reaction to a low-flying patrol plane flown over Tsavo National Park by Warden Patrick Hamilton. This defense mechanism, while effective in nature, plays into the hands of poachers armed with automatic rifles.

poorly equipped anti-poaching units. In Kenya, for example, poachers in the late 1980s were using assault rifles against game rangers armed with ancient World War II British rifles. Some rangers were armed only with small-caliber .22 rifles, the sort used in the United States for hunting rabbits and squirrels. The rangers' worn out motor vehicles rarely ran and, when they did, there was no gasoline to be put in them.

Ivory that left Africa in recent years was destined for a number of ports. Those handling some of the largest quantities in the 1980s were known for their laxity at enforcing CITES regulations. The biggest entrepots were Hong Kong, Taiwan, Japan, and the United Arab Emirates. Carving factories in the United Arab Emirates "legalized" thousands of tons of poached *raw* ivory by crudely cutting it so that it would qualify as *worked* ivory. This process took advantage of a loophole in the CITES Ivory Control System. Under the system, trade restrictions covered only raw ivory, while worked ivory is automatically treated as legal. By definition, worked ivory is any tusk that has been cut into pieces or even mounted on a wooden board. From the United Arab Emirates and other Middle Eastern nations, tons of crudely cut ivory were shipped to Singapore, Hong Kong, China, and Japan for final carving—ivory that represented the lives of hundreds of thousands of illegally killed elephants.

Singapore in the mid-1980s imported increasing amounts of ivory, reaching some 300 tons in 1986. The burgeoning trade occurred at least in part because it was known among ivory merchants that CITES would be legalizing poached ivory in 1986 to clear the market. In November of that year, CITES legalized the 300 tons stored in Singapore, yielding millions of dollars to traders literally over night. Legalization was supposed to make it easier to control the ivory trade, but in fact it seems only to have stimulated a vast poaching effort.

Among the traders who benefited from the legalization were Poon Tat Wah, known as George, and Poon Tat Hong. The Poon brothers made nearly $8 million when the value of the ivory they had stockpiled in Singapore skyrocketed after it was legalized. George Poon lives in Paris, where he has an ivory carving shop, one of many Poon-brothers shops scattered across the globe. Poon Tat Hong lives in Hong Kong, where for many years he organized ivory imports and sales. The brothers also had ivory factories in the United Arab Emirates, Hong Kong, Taiwan, Macau, and Singapore in addition to factories in France.

Another ivory trading family that benefited from the Singapore ivory amnesty was the Lai family of Hong Kong. Headed by Mi-

In some areas of Tsavo National Park, killing grounds are littered with skeletons of poached elephants. Here some 24 were slaughtered in 1988, a year of rampant poaching.

chael Lai, the family owns ivory-carving factories in Hong Kong and Singapore. Lai Yu Key, Michael Lai's nephew, admitted in a 1989 interview that the family established a factory in Singapore to evade trade controls on ivory. They have exported raw ivory to the United States, Japan, Taiwan, and Europe. Brochures about their operations boasted that the Lai's Kee Cheong Ivory Factory could produce 30,000 ivory bangles, 40,000 bracelets, and 100,000 rings monthly.

The world's leading ivory trader was probably K.T. Wang, who has strong connections to French-speaking Africa, which encompasses the regions that are home to forest elephants. He had more than 150 tons of ivory stockpiled in Singapore at the time of the amnesty and, on the last day of the amnesty, imported more than 10 tons of ivory from Burundi. In 1990 Wang was in his sixties. He had been one of the biggest ivory dealers in the world since the 1970s but had never been to Africa or seen an elephant out-side of a zoo. He had, however, engineered ivory deals not only for himself but for others as well. In 1987 he helped an Osaka dealer buy 26 tons of ivory from Congo, some 2,000 tusks valued at $3.5 million. In 1989 he helped Tokyo's largest trader, Koichiro

(OPPOSITE)
A big, rust-red bull feeds in the rain in Tsavo East National Park. Since mature bulls are prime poacher targets, he will be lucky to reach a ripe old age of 60.

The carcass of an elephant killed by poachers in 1990 in Tsavo East National Park resembles a tent. Poachers often cover a kill with bushes to prevent immediate detection.

Kitagawa, purchase nearly 5 tons of Sudanese ivory for $1 million.

The massive amounts of ivory that were moving through the markets—more than 1,000 tons yearly in the 1980s, compared to 200 tons in the 1950s when average tusk size was larger—made it clear that CITES controls were failing. Lack of enforcement capability and poor monitoring contributed to the failure. But there was also some concern that CITES officials were unduly influenced by the traders themselves, since the traders contributed large sums of money to help fund operations of the CITES Ivory Control System. Between 1985 and 1989, fully two-thirds of the budget was provided by ivory dealers. Japan's ivory-trade association contributed $140,000 of the $237,000 that came from ivory traders. K. T. Wang donated $10,000 right after his ivory stock was legalized by the 1986 amnesty and gave another $20,000 in 1988. CITES officials maintained that they had no other adequate funding source and that, since the ivory traders had a vested interest in how they were regulated, they made willing donors. But the potential conflict of interest is plain in a situation in which the regulators' salaries are dependent upon funds from the people being regulated. Clearly something else needed to be done.

▌ THE IVORY TRADE BAN: SAVING ELEPHANTS AT THE CASH REGISTER

In light of CITES obvious failure to control the ivory trade, individual nations stepped in. In May 1988 the African Wildlife Foundation, based in Washington, D.C., launched a campaign to end the ivory trade. In the months that followed, much of the foundation's efforts came to fruition. In September 1988 the U.S. Congress enacted the African Elephant Conservation Act, authorizing the secretary of the Interior to prohibit the import of ivory from any nation dealing in illegal ivory and from any nation that does not adhere to CITES. As a result, ivory imports from Chad, Ethiopia, Gabon, and Somalia were immediately outlawed. In addition the law banned the import of ivory from nations that act as intermediaries for African nations exporting tusks. The following June the United States—which imported $18 million to $26 million worth of worked ivory yearly in the 1980s, accounting for 10 to 12 percent of world trade—announced a complete ban on commercial ivory imports. The same month Japan announced a ban on the import of worked and raw ivory and ivory scraps from nations that do not produce their own ivory. The following September Japan initiated a ban on all ivory imports regardless of the nation of origin. Japan's ban is even stricter than that of the United States, prohibiting, for example, the import of elephant trophies by sport hunters. Such trophies can still be brought into the United States from Zimbabwe and South Africa.

But the African nations that were hard-hit by poaching did not believe that such nation-by-nation bans were enough. Surveys showed that the ivory trade was killing elephants at about 20 times the rate that the elephant population could sustain. The hardest-hit African nations believed this could be stopped only by an international ban on all commerce in ivory. Consequently Tanzania, at the CITES meeting held in October 1989, asked that the African elephant be moved to Appendix I, which would ban all commercial trade in ivory. Kenya, as hard hit as Tanzania, favored the international ban, as did eight other African nations and many other non-African nations, including the United States.

Opposed to the ban were the countries of southern Africa— Zimbabwe, Zambia, South Africa, Botswana, Malawi, and Namibia, all of which maintained that they had stable or increasing elephant populations. Their representatives argued that the east African nations should come to southern Africa to learn how to properly manage and protect wildlife. They said that if a ban were placed on the ivory trade, the southern African nations would be penalized with financial losses even though they have managed their elephants well. Moreover the ivory trade would be forced underground, into the black market, where it would be impossible to monitor. A ban on ivory trade, they said, would raise the price of tusks and lead to widespread elephant slaughter, much as a ban on trade in rhino horn had led to a massacre of rhinos as prices for horn skyrocketed. In addition, farmers who suffer when elephants raid their crops would turn against the elephant if they could make no money from its ivory. For example, the killing of elephants in 1988 in a single district in Zimbabwe netted the district government $125,000. If the ivory trade were halted, elephants would switch from being a protected cash crop to being mere varmints to be destroyed because they ruin crops. On top of all that, the southern African nations maintained that they had too many elephants, that they needed to cull herds to keep them from overpopulating.

Ban proponents argued that a complete prohibition on ivory trade was the only way to save the elephant. They pointed out that African nations garner little money from the ivory trade— less than 10 percent of the $60 million in legal trade reaches national coffers. The value of elephant-related tourism in Kenya alone is about $200 million, more than 30 times what the entire continent makes from dead elephants. Poached ivory, they said, is a complete loss to African economies. Ban proponents claimed that the elephant problem was not a national but a continental problem. Once poachers had killed off the elephants of central and east Africa, they would turn their guns to the better-protected animals of southern Africa.

Those in favor of the ban argued that poaching of elephants and trade in ivory could not be compared to the poaching of rhinos and trade in rhino horn, which nearly wiped out the black and white rhinos. Rhino horn was bought for the Oriental medical trade and for making handles on the special daggers that symbolize manhood in Yemen. Worked ivory is sold mainly in developed nations such as the United States and Japan, where it is used for luxury items. The elephant problem, ban proponents said, should be compared not to that of the rhino but to that of spotted cats, such as the leopard. Leopards were threatened with extinction in the 1960s and 1970s because their hides were in big demand for high-fashion coats and other garments. When the leopard's plight became known in the developed world, a ban was placed on trade in spotted cat furs, and the animal has since substantially recovered.

Members of one bond-group feed on lush, rainy-season grass after slapping mud on their bodies. Lack of poaching in Amboseli, where these elephants live, has preserved their social bonds. It is not likely that a single elephant in parks hard hit by poaching is living under normal social conditions.

As for farmers slaughtering crop-eating elephants, the proponents pointed out that most of the elephant range in east and central Africa had not been as heavily farmed as the ranges in southern Africa. The problem was poachers, pure and simple. And if the southern nations had too many elephants—and these nations have produced little scientific evidence to support this claim—they could cull them whether or not there was an ivory trade. After all, the southern goverments always maintained that the culls were conducted for biological, not economic, reasons. Lack of ivory exports should not stifle biologically induced culls. As for Kenya, Tanzania, and other African nations adopting the management policies of southern Africa, proponents said it was economically impossible. These nations lacked the strong economies of southern Africa and could not afford the personnel and equipment needed for more intensive management. A Zambian study indicated that it would cost about $1 per acre to protect elephants adequately in parks. With one of Africa's best conservation programs, Zimbabwe has never spent more than 80 cents per acre. Most of Africa invests no more than a quarter of a cent per acre.

The proponents won their ban, though China, Zimbabwe, Zambia, Botswana, South Africa, and Mozambique announced intentions to ignore it, and Burundi announced that it still wanted to sell nearly 90 tons of stockpiled ivory. There was also widespread consternation when Great Britain allowed its protectorate, Hong Kong, six months to export several hundred tons of stockpiled ivory despite the ban.

Nevertheless the unilateral moratorium and the international ban, coupled with increasingly tough anti-poaching measures in Kenya and Tanzania, had tremendous results within months. Ivory prices soon fell. Ivory that was sold in Somalia for up to $35 a pound in 1989 was being offered for as little as $1 a pound, with no takers. In the Central African Republic, prices fell by as much as 70 percent within six months after the ban. In Zaire prices fell 60 to 85 percent. In South Africa the government sold raw ivory for $150 a pound in January 1989, but 10 months later failed to receive a single bid when it offered to sell 1.3 tons. Other nations that found no buyers for ivory were Burundi, Namibia, the Central African Republic, and Yemen. An auction planned by Zimbabwe, Botswana, and South Africa was cancelled because of lack of interest.

A World Wildlife Fund survey in May 1990 of the 15 largest wholesale ivory dealers in the United States found that ivory sales began to decline in early 1989, months before the official ban, because of public concern about elephant survival. After the ban consumer demand for ivory virtually dried up. Prices for ivory jewelry and simple carvings, traditionally the bulk of the trade, were down 40 to 70 percent. High-quality carvings were off 5 to 10 percent. Hawaii, the largest U.S. wholesale market, saw nearly a complete collapse in ivory sales. Demand, said one New York dealer, no longer exists.

In Japan prices for raw ivory did skyrocket immediately after the import ban, quadrupling to nearly $400 per pound. But prices for ivory products, after this initial leap, started to decline in 1990 as the Japanese became more aware of the elephant's plight. By

Detail of a carved tusk. The international ivory ban enacted in 1990 has nearly shut down the oriental carving factories that produced such work.

spring 1990 many of Japan's leading department stores, including the famous Mitsukoshi stores, were cutting back on ivory sales as demand fell off.

In Hong Kong most retailers left the ivory business in the months after the ban or diversified into other ventures. About 75 percent of Hong Kong's 2,000 ivory carvers gave up their craft, and the government prepared to retrain them for other work. Retail prices for ivory products dropped off by 20 to 40 percent, and the wholesale price of ivory fell 15 to 20 percent.

China was the only non-African nation to refuse the ban. Though China had little money for ivory imports, it could help keep poaching alive. African nations feared that China would become a market for poached ivory. Nevertheless in the months following the ban, the Chinese ivory industry collapsed, leaving carving factories working at less than 5 percent capacity. The factories laid off hundreds of workers. A Beijing factory, formerly one of the largest, employed only five of 550 workers by mid-1990. Canton's Daxin Factory, the second largest, still had at work in early 1990 only one of the 400 carvers who were turning out ivory products in mid-1989. The failing ivory factories reportedly were paying workers 75 percent of their salaries *not* to carve ivory. In early September 1990, China announced that it would withdraw its reservation on the ban on January 1, 1991.

Taiwan, though not a CITES member, supported the ban. The government seized shipments from Hong Kong, and in May 1990 publicly burned nearly 800 pounds of confiscated wildlife products, including raw and worked ivory.

Evidence suggests that poaching is declining in some parts of Africa after the ban was initiated, but the decline cannot be attributed to the ban alone. The African nations have stepped up law enforcement efforts. In Kenya, Richard Leakey, a Kenyan citizen and son of the famous paleontologists Louis and Mary Leakey, was named head of the nation's Wildlife Services in spring 1989. Given a free hand by President Daniel arap Moi, he immediately initiated changes in administration and personnel, weeding out corrupt officials and park rangers. He traveled abroad, raising funds for his department, including a donation by one individual of $200,000 for gasoline. He also persuaded the government to allow his department to keep some of the $300 million in foreign exchange yearly that comes in from fees paid at parks and resorts. The department's miserly $7 million budget was thus given an influx of fresh cash. Moreover, park entrance fees have been raised under Leakey's administration.

Leakey, with the blessing of the Kenyan government, has mod-

Rangers patrol the Aruba Dam area of Tsavo East National Park. Tsavo, once a prime target of poachers, is patrolled on the ground and from the air. Stepped up surveillance under Richard Leakey cut poaching in the park to zero within months.

Warden Patrick Hamilton, on aerial patrol over Tsavo National Park, takes a closer look for signs of poachers. He and Warden Joseph Kioko each log about 100 airborne hours a month. The army flies additional helicopter patrols over the park.

ernized his forces, equipping game rangers with automatic rifles, boots, uniforms, communications equipment, and daily allowances. With a bigger budget, he is able to offer rewards to people who provide information that leads to poachers, their weapons, or poached ivory. He also has doubled the rangers' salaries.

In the seven months following Leakey's appointment, 60 poachers were killed or captured and 500 tusks were confiscated. In October 1989 Kenyan forces killed Mohamed Hussein Omar, said to be the leader of a gang that had poached around Meru National Park and the man thought to have killed two French tourists there in July 1989, as well as a game ranger and a tour guide in 1988. One measure of the success of these actions is that by 1990 poaching in Kenya had nearly come to a halt. In 1988 about two elephants were killed every day in Tsavo National Park. None were killed there in the opening months of Leakey's administration, though 14 were poached about 50 miles south of the park.

Much of this success has stemmed from the vast improvement in Kenya's anti-poaching forces. In addition to being better equipped, the nations' anti-poaching forces are also better trained. They receive nine months of paramilitary training, learning both police and military tactics, and a year of training in wildlife management. In addition, all rangers are native Africans chosen for physical fitness and prowess in the field. "These people are very bush-wise," Leakey says.

The rangers constantly patrol the parks, going out on week-long forays. They begin their patrols at dawn, looking for any sign of poachers—tracks, abandoned campsites, even the behavior of elephant groups. If the herds seem peaceful and calm, it is safe to presume that no poachers are about. But if the animals are skittish, jumpy, on edge, the rangers go on the alert for a possible confrontation with poachers.

Because the anti-poaching patrols are aligned against heavily armed poachers, they conduct themselves as would any military unit fighting guerilla insurgents. As does any infantry, the rangers carry their own food and water. They also carry medical supplies in case of casualties and are trained for air evacuation. Backup supplies are carried in the motor vehicles with which the rangers usually meet when they bivouac for the night. Daily patrols end a little before nightfall, though on moonlit nights, when poachers may operate, the rangers continue surveillance.

In the first six months of 1990, poaching came nearly to a standstill. Though about 75 poachers were killed during the first 14 months of Leakey's administration—compared to perhaps a

dozen in the year before Leakey assumed office—most of those deaths occurred during the first six months, Leakey said. By increasing the risks of poaching at the same time that world markets stopped trading ivory, Kenya has made poachers less eager to go afield, Leakey said.

Government action also seems to be stemming the actions of poachers along southern Sudan, where military units from the Central African Republic have begun patroling the border with Sudan. A professional hunter in the area said that several hundred elephants were killed there yearly before the patrols started. Only 20 elephants were killed in 1989, the year the patrols began, and none in the first five months of 1990.

An elephant pauses from feeding among shrubs and bushes to test the air, holding his trunk high to detect danger. Elephant behavior sometimes tips off game rangers to the presence of poachers. If a herd is calm, all is probably well. If the animals are nervous and easily frightened, poachers may be lurking nearby after a recent kill.

Poaching continues in Zaire, though data is hard to find, and the southern African nations report little organized poaching.

▊ THE ROCKY ROAD AHEAD

Although there is reason for optimism about African elephant survival, the future for the elephant is still uncertain. The southern African nations have announced intentions to continue trade in ivory, saying that they will sell only to approved and registered manufacturers. However, some conservationists believe that any trade in ivory will revive the wanton poaching that has killed more than half of Africa's elephants in the past 15 years. Certainly trade of any sort will make it difficult to control the sale of poached ivory, since no proven means exists for accurately determining from which nation an ivory product came.

New forensic techniques are being developed that could help to solve this problem. One technique involves examining the DNA of soft tissues, such as muscle, that might be attached to a tusk. If certain DNA types can be clearly linked to certain elephant populations, it would be possible to use DNA as a sort of fingerprint that shows where the ivory originated. Another, perhaps more promising, technique involves chemical identification of tusks. People working on this technique reason that elephants in different parts of Africa have different diets and that the diets influence chemical traces found in tusks. For example, elephants that eat mostly grasses show higher levels of the carbon-13 isotope than do those that eat mostly trees and shrubs. By determining what isotopes turn up in tusks and by analyzing plant foods from various areas, scientists might be able to develop a means for identifying tusk origins. Researchers have already determined that tusks from Kenya's Tsavo National Park have a different chemical fingerprint from tusks collected at Shimba Hills National Park, only 50 miles away.

The clearest defense for elephants, as the success of the international trade ban shows, is a lack of consumer demand. Ivory cannot be collected without killing elephants, so demand for ivory will always compel the death of elephants. The slaughter of the African elephant begins not in the African bush, but in the homes and businesses of Europe, the United States, Japan, and other ivory-hungry nations.

Poaching as a threat to elephant survival probably can be stopped, says Richard Leakey. However, he adds, poaching is just part of the elephants' problem. Looming ominously in the future

(OPPOSITE)
A British freelance photographer lays out tusks and leg traps recovered from poachers in Tsavo East National Park. He was traveling with several journalists doing articles on anti-poaching efforts in Kenya.

His tusks and ears scarred through the years, this male pauses from his feeding routine. His broken tusks will grow throughout his lifetime, even making a spurt in his last decade. The oldest animals bear the biggest tusks. If ivory were collected only from elephants that died of natural causes, in a few years Africa could produce three times as much ivory as can be taken from animals shot for tusks, says David Western, East African regional director of Wildlife Conservation International. This is because poachers quickly kill off the big animals and then turn to killing youngsters with tiny tusks.

is a much more complex challenge—the need for a place where elephants can live unmolested.

Africa has the world's fastest growing human population. As people swarm across the continent, they destroy wildlife habitat and replace it with farms, villages, and cities. This leaves little room for wildlife. In the near future, elephants may find themselves trapped in a world in which farm crops are the only food sources outside of parks. To keep their numbers within the carrying capacity of the parks, governments may cull the herds. If the elephants move off the parks, they will quite likely be shot by farmers or government hunters hired to protect crops. Africa, in the near future, will be faced with the increasingly difficult challenge of managing both people and wildlife. Already in Kenya, whose 4 percent yearly birthrate is the world's largest, people crowd against the borders of some parks. When the nation's population doubles by the end of the century, will the government finally yield to demands that the parks be opened to human development? Or will the government protect the parks because tourism is so essential to the economy?

Another problem is political and economic instability. Revolutions and warfare bring more firearms into the continent, and the firearms often are turned against wildlife. If a market for ivory exists, then the sale of ivory to finance revolutionary organizations will threaten some elephant populations. For example, Colonel Jan Breytenbach, a senior South African Defense Force officer who fought in Angola, has reported that pro-Western Angolan guerrillas with whom he lived and worked have killed thousands of elephants to finance their war against Angola's Marxist goverment. And under the trigger-happy regime of Idi Amin, Uganda lost thousands of elephants. Amin's soldiers wiped out all but 160 of the 8,000 elephants that lived in Kabalega Falls National Park. Warfare also can lead to wholesale slaughter of wildlife when beseiged governments can no longer protect parks and wilderness regions.

Protecting elephants into even the foreseeable future is a difficult task with a dubious outcome. But the African Elephant Conservation Coordinating Group—a panel of biologists formed in 1988 to help ensure elephant recovery and funded primarily by the World Wildlife Fund-U.S., the U.S. Fish and Wildlife Service, and the European Economic Community—has developed a plan. It has targeted 49 key elephant populations, ranging from 150 to 29,000 animals, in various parts of Africa whose protection the group believes is essential to elephant survival. It may be that these are the only elephants that *can* be saved if poaching contin-

The Maasai serve as unofficial game rangers in parks like Amboseli. They report poachers and leave wild animals unmolested, because a large part of their income depends on wildlife and tourism. As livestock raisers they have little interest in wild game. However, they are switching gradually from raising cattle to growing crops, which may lead to increasing conflicts with wildlife.

ues. The total number is less than 220,000, roughly a third of the elephants alive today.

This is a grim prospect and a sad commentary on the world that human society is creating. Richard Leakey, in fact, thinks that the coordinating group has set its sights too low. Existing parks, he believes, could support some 700,000 elephants and, he says, this is the goal toward which elephant conservationists should work. But achieving even this scant number will require implementation of several intensive conservation measures outlined by the coordinating group. Anti-poaching actions will have to be stepped up. Better controls on trade in elephant products will have to be initiated. Each elephant population and elephant-range nation will need a distinct management plan, requiring vast

amounts of scientific research and administration. The public—particularly peoples living within elephant range—will have to be made more aware of the elephant's plight and of the human role in creating that plight. And finally, extensive research must be conducted on elephant behavior, movement patterns, habitat use, and population dynamics.

Europe, the United States, and Japan will need to play a critical role in protecting the African elephant. These nations were the economic power behind the poachers who nearly wiped out the elephant, and they need to rectify the destruction wrought by their consumption. The best way to do this is by funding elephant conservation programs in Africa. Clearly the African nations,

Native African people may be a blessing or a curse to park wildlife. They often help game rangers locate poachers and report poaching activities. But as Africans turn from raising livestock to growing crops, conflicts with wildlife are increasing along park borders. Kenya Wildlife Service director Richard Leakey proposes extensive fencing along some borders to keep wildlife out of croplands.

Part of a large herd hesitates, cut off from cohorts by tourists eager to get elephant photographs with a Mt. Kilimanjaro backdrop. After minutes of indecision, the herd cautiously crossed the road. As a major tourist attraction and income generator, elephants are key contributors to the health of many African national economies.

drowning in a growing sea of humanity and poverty, cannot by themselves finance elephant protection, cannot meet the expense of solving a problem that the markets of the developed world created. In the years ahead, without outside help, they may feel forced to trade wildlife for the momentary relief that a few new farms may bring.

The developed nations are already funding some elephant conservation. For example, the U.S. Congress in the African Elephant Conservation Act authorized $5 million yearly for the task. But Congress has been slow to provide those funds. In 1989 only $500,000—a tenth the authorized amount, about one thirty-second of the value of the ivory sold in the United States every year in the 1980s—was appropriated. Moreover, the authorized amount is miniscule in proportion to the need for funds: The Ken-

A (OPPOSITE) young adult brings a fresh-cropped trunkful to its mouth. Elephants in some areas eat some 700 pounds of grass and other greenery daily, but dumpsites in national parks have lured some to a change of diet and claimed at least one victim in Amboseli, found with hundreds of beercaps in its stomach. Tourism gives African nations an economic reason for protecting wildlife, but is clearly a double-edged sword if not carefully managed.

191

yan Wildlife Service alone will need an estimated $200 million during the next five years.

Private citizens, acting through organizations such as the World Wildlife Fund, have proved more generous than their governments. The wildlife fund spent nearly $3 million on elephant conservation in nine African nations in 1990. Private citizens concerned about the elephant should let their governments know how they feel and urge them to provide better funding for elephant protection. Money should be spent not just to quell poaching—though clearly at the moment that is the most important issue—but also to study elephants and their habitat needs and to acquire proper lands that can be managed and protected for them in the future.

Despite all the obstacles arrayed against elephant survival, some hope remains. That hope glimmers most brightly in India, where a commitment to elephant protection has cut poaching to the bone and provided elephants with havens against human development. What has happened in India is a clear sign that a nation committed to conservation can beat even seemingly impossible odds.

India is home to a different species of elephant, the Asian or Indian elephant. It differs from the African elephant in a number of obvious physical traits. Its ears are smaller, its forehead is more bulbous, and its back is arched rather than swayed. The Asian elephant's tusks tend to be smaller, and cows often lack tusks altogether. The trunks differ, too. The Asian elephant has only one finger-like appendage at the tip of its trunk, while the African has two.

The Asian elephant once ranged from Syria to Southeast Asia. Small numbers still roam Vietnam and Thailand, but the elephant was wiped out at the other end of its range in Classical times.

About 30,000 to 40,000 Asian elephants survive out of perhaps 20 times that number a century ago. They have been victims primarily of habitat loss. As the forests that they favor have been cut, they have been pressed into smaller and smaller areas, their numbers declining.

But they have not fallen victim to poachers as African elephants have, even though India counts some 2,000 ivory craftsmen among its work force. This is particularly interesting because ivory bangles are considered an essential part of an Indian woman's wardrobe, the more bangles the better.

India joined CITES in 1976 and in the process outlawed the export of items made from Asian elephant ivory. But since ivory was still sold legally within the nation, much of it was smuggled out. When smuggling led to increased poaching in the early 1980s, India in November 1986 ended all commercial use of local ivory. In 1988 it dropped all import duties on African ivory, which lowered the price of African ivory and stimulated African poaching, but deterred poaching in India.

Despite the elimination of import duties on African ivory, India did not ignore the plight of the African elephant. As early as 1986, India required all ivory factories, dealers, and individual craftsman to obtain annual licenses and to submit monthly reports on the amounts of raw African ivory purchased and on the number of pieces made, their weights, and the number sold. These ivory-trade regulations are among the toughest in the world, and they are enforced by inspectors who visit shops and craftsmen's houses. In fact the regulations were so tough that nearly three-quarters of India's craftsmen left the ivory business and began carving camel bones or the bones of domestic livestock. They also switched to wood, particularly sandalwood, and some carvers have learned to cut gems.

The Indian government recognized that the regulations were hard on the ivory industry, but felt that elephant survival was more important. Poaching had posed a serious threat to the nation's elephants. In southern India, from 1980 to 1986, at least 100 elephants were killed each year from a population of 6,500. In late 1986 one poaching gang killed at least 15 bull elephants within a short period.

Official response to the poachers involved more than regulating trade. The forestry departments of four heavily poached states in southern India combined their resources and coordinated their efforts. They obtained communications equipment, modernized their firearms, and expanded their intelligence operations. The last was crucial to locating the poachers, which they did in 1987. The leader escaped the ensuing shoot-out but was never seen in the area again, though his name was put on a wanted list. After his disappearance, elephant numbers in the area increased.

With one of the lowest per-capita incomes in the world and the second largest human population, India has managed its elephants, tigers, and rhinos with such success that the animals' populations are stable or increasing. India has done this by adopting the measures that Richard Leakey is applying in Kenya and that other African nations are also initiating. The Indian forestry department obtained the necessary law-enforcement equipment and built morale among all its personnel, committing them to wildlife protection. With no money from other nations and little advice from foreign experts, India has strictly enforced ivory

An adult chews the branches of a fallen acacia tree. Elephants often knock down trees before stripping the bark and branches. They also eat seedlings, retarding the regrowth of woodlands. Many scientists believe that this is part of a long-term, natural cycle of growth and destruction.

trade regulations, and its forestry department has worked to improve its ability to gather intelligence, a critical element in dealing with poachers.

Though India offers some encouragement for those seeking protection for the African elephant, the elephant's future in Africa is far from certain. Human greed will never abate. As long as a single African elephant survives, there will be someone willing to kill it for personal gain. But the poachers do not act alone. They are merely the agents of those who buy ivory products in the shops of Europe, Asia, and North America. If poaching continues at the level of the 1980s, elephant populations will vanish or be reduced to a tattered, unapproachable, frightened remnant within the next 15 years. If this happens the blame must be borne by consumers of ivory products. "The elephant," said Oria Douglas-Hamilton during her 1989 fund-raising tour of the United States, "is being destroyed just so we can have trinkets to put in our drawers."

Those who want the elephant to survive cannot hesitate any longer to seek support for the elephant and a permanent end to the killing of elephants for ivory. The refusal of consumers to participate in the carnage is the African elephant's only chance for a future.

"Thirty thousand elephants: three hundred tons of ivory, if that. And as the aim of good government is to increase production, I'm sure that this year we shall do better. Let us not forget that the Belgian Congo alone has supplied more than sixty thousand elephants in the last few years; their last official figure is seven thousand a year—but would you hesitate to say it's closer to ten thousand? I'm sure we shall all put our hearts into surpassing this record. With a little good will, we shall certainly manage, taking Africa as a whole, to kill a hundred thousand elephants a year, and so on till the ceiling is reached, if I may put it that way. It will then be necessary to pass to other species. Ours, I suggest."

Romain Gary, *The Roots of Heaven*, 1958

REFERENCES

█ RECOMMENDED READING

Bull, Bartle. 1988. *Safari: A Chronicle of Adventure*. Viking. London.

Bryce, James. 1900. *Impressions of South Africa*. The Century Co. New York.

Carrington, Richard. 1959. *Elephants: A Short Account of their Natural History, Evolution, and Influence on Mankind*. Basic Books, Inc. New York.

Douglas-Hamilton, Iain and Oria. 1975. *Among the Elephants*. The Viking Press. New York.

Lamb, David. 1982. *The Africans*. Random House. New York.

Moss, Cynthia. 1988. *Elephant Memories: Thirteen Years in the Life of an Elephant Family*. Fawcett Columbine. New York.

Roosevelt, Kermit. 1963. *A Sentimental Safari*. Alfred A. Knopf. New York.

Roosevelt, Theodore. 1909. *African Game Trails*. Syndicate Publishing Co. New York.

Savage, R.J.G. 1986. *Mammal Evolution, An Illustrated Guide*. Facts on File Publications. New York.

Scullard, H.H. 1974. *The Elephant in the Greek and Roman World*. Cornell University Press. Ithaca, New York.

Sikes, Sylvia. 1971. *The Natural History of the African Elephant*. American Elsebier Publishing Co., Inc.

Sillar, F.C. and R.M. Meyler. 1968. *Elephants, Ancient and Modern*. Viking Press. New York.

Silverberg, Robert. 1967. *The Morning of Mankind: Prehistoric Man in Europe*. New York Graphic Society Publishers, Ltd.

———. 1970. *Mammoths, Mastodons, and Man*. McGraw-Hill Book Company. New York.

Williams, Heathcote. 1989. *Sacred Elephant*. Jonathan Cape. London.

Wilson, Derek and Peter Ayerst. 1976. *White Gold: The Story of African Ivory*. Taplinger Publishing Company. New York.

█ OTHER REFERENCES

Anonymous. 1989. "The Ivory Trade Threatens Africa's Elephants." African Wildlife Foundation. Washington, D.C.

Armstrong, Sue and Fred Bridgland. 1989. "Elephants and the ivory tower." *New Scientist* 26 Aug.:37.

Barnes, Richard and Karen. 1990. "You can't see the elephants for the trees." *Wildlife Conservation* March/April:38–45.

Burchell, William J. 1937. *Selections From Travels in the Interior of Southern Africa.* Oxford University Press. London.

Bohlen, Janet Trowbridge. 1989. "Africa's ivory war." *Defenders* Mar./Apr.:10.

Eltringham, S.K. 1982. *Elephants.* Blandford Press. Poole, Dorret, England.

Fage, J.D. 1979. *A History of Africa.* Alfred A. Knopf. New York.

Guillet, Alfredo. 1990. "Ivory smuggling in Sudan." *Swara* Jan./Feb.:31.

Hanks, John. 1979. *The Struggle for Survival: The Elephant Problem.* Mayflower Books. New York.

Harris, William Cornwallis. 1852. *The Wild Sports of Southern Africa.* Henry G. Bohn. London.

Hemingway, Ernest. 1935. *Green Hills of Africa.* Charles Scribner's Sons. New York.

Hotchner, A.E. 1989. *Hemingway and His World.* The Vendome Press. New York.

Jewell, Peter A. and Sidney Holt, eds. 1981. *Problems in Management of Locally Abundant Wild Mammals.* Academic Press. New York.

Livy. 1988. *The War with Hannibal.* Penguin Books. London.

Lydekker, Richard. 1896. *The New Natural History.* Merrill & Baker. New York.

Martin, Esmond Bradley. 1990. "Ivory and elephants in India." *Swara* Jan./Feb.:26.

Martin, Phyllis M. and Patrick O'Meara. 1977. *Africa.* Indiana University Press. Bloomington.

O'Connell, Michael A. and Michael Sutton. 1990. "The Effects of Trade Moratoria on International Commerce in African Elephant Ivory: A Preliminary Report." World Wildlife Fund and The Conservation Foundation. Washington, D.C.

Oliver, Roland and Michael Crowder, eds. 1981. *The Cambridge Encyclopedia of Africa.* Cambridge University Press.

Poole, Joyce H. 1987. "Rutting behavior in African elephants: the phenomenon of musth." *Behaviour* 102:283–316.

———, Katherine Payne, William R. Langbauer Jr., and Cynthia Moss. 1988. "The social contexts of some very low frequency calls of African elephants." *Behavioral Ecology and Sociobiology* 22:385–392.

———. 1989. "Announcing intent: the aggressive state of musth in African elephants." *Animal Behaviour* 37:140–152.

———. 1989. "Mate guarding, reproductive success and female choice in African elephants." *Animal Behaviour* 37:842–849.

ILLUSTRATION CREDITS

The author gratefully acknowledges the following for photographs and artwork reproduced in this book:

Neg. No. 310830 (Photo by Kirschner), page 6, courtesy Department of Library Sciences, American Museum of Natural History

The Bettmann Archive, pages 7, 9, 10, 19, 22, 24, 25, 150

Christopher L. Brest, page 14, adapted from United Nations Environment Programme data, compiled during a 15-year study by Iain Douglas-Hamilton, and maps by Fran Michelmore and Todd Treadway / Hellman Associates, Inc.

The Library of Congress, pages 16, 54, 148

The Granger Collection, New York, pages 21, 37, 39

Camerapix / Duncan Willets, pages 140, 141

Rick Weyerhaeuser / World Wildlife Fund, page 153

© 1989, Washington Post Writers Group, page 164

Katherine Payne/World Wildlife Fund, page 166

INDEX

Bold face pages refer to illustrations